The Parable of
The Wicked Mammon

by
William Tyndale

That faith, the mother of all good works, justifieth us, before we can bring forth any good work : as the husband marrieth his wife before he can have any lawful children by her. Furthermore, as the husband marrieth not his wife that she should continue unfruitful as before, and as she was in the state of virginity, (wherein it was impossible for her to bear fruit) but contrariwise to make her fruitful ; even so faith justifieth us not, that is to say, marrieth us not to God, that we should continue unfruitful as before, but that he should put the seed of his Holy Spirit in us, (as St. John in his first Epistle calleth it) and to make us fruitful. For, saith Paul, (Eph. ii.) "By grace are ye made safe through faith, and that not of yourselves : for it is the gift of God, and cometh not of the works, lest any man should boast himself. For we are his workmanship, created in Christ Jesus unto good works, which God hath ordained that we should walk in them." Amen.

WILLIAM TYNDALE,

OTHERWISE CALLED HITCHINS,

TO THE READER.

———

GRACE and peace, with all manner [of] spiritual feeling and living, worthy of the kindness of Christ, be with the reader, and with all that trust the will of God. Amen.

The cause why I set my name before this little Treatise, and have not rather done it in the New Testament, is, that then I followed the the counsel of Christ, which exhorteth men (Matt. vi.) to do their good deeds secretly, and to be content with the conscience of well-doing; and that God seeth us; and patiently to abide the reward of the last day, which Christ hath purchased for us: and now would I fain have done likewise, but am I compelled otherwise to do.

The cause why W. Tyndale put his name to some books, and left it out in some.

While I abode, a faithful companion, which now hath taken another voyage upon him, to preach Christ where, I suppose, he was never yet preached, (God, which put in his heart thither to go, send his Spirit with him, comfort him, and bring his purpose to good effect,) one William Roye, a man somewhat crafty, when he cometh unto new acquaintance, and before he be thorough known, and namely, when all is

William Roye a false disciple.

spent, came unto me and offered his help. As
long as he had no money somewhat I could
rule him; but as soon as he had gotten him
money, he became like himself again. Nevertheless, I suffered all things till that was ended,
which I could not do alone without one, both to
write, and to help me to compare the texts
together. When that was ended, I took my
leave, and bade him farewell for our two lives;
and, as men say, a day longer. After we were
departed, he went and gat him new friends,
which thing to do he passeth all that ever I yet
knew. And there, when he had stored him of
money, he gat him to Argentine, where he professeth wonderful faculties, and maketh boast of
no small things. A year after that, and now
twelve months before the printing of this work,

Jerome a
brother of
Greenwich.

came one Jerome, a brother of Greenwich also,
through Worms to Argentine, saying that he in-
tended to be Christ's disciple another while, and
to keep (as nigh as God would give him grace,)
the profession of his baptism, and to get his
living with his hands, and to live no longer idly,
and of the sweat and labour of those captives,
which they had taught not to believe in Christ,
but in cut shoes, and russet coats. Which
Jerome, with all diligence, I warned of Roye's
boldness, and exhorted him to beware of him,
and to walk quietly, and with all patience and
long-suffering, according as we have Christ and
his apostles for an ensample, which thing he also
promised me.

Nevertheless, when he was come to Argentine, William Roye (whose tongue is able not only to make fools stark mad, but also to deceive the wisest, that is at the first sight and acquaintance,) gat him to him, and set him a work to make rhymes, while he himself translated a dialogue out of Latin into English, in whose Prologue he promiseth more a great deal than I fear me he will ever pay.   Paul saith, (2 Tim. ii.) *2 Tim. ii.* " The servant of the Lord must not strive, but be peaceable unto all men, and ready to teach, and one that can suffer the evil with meekness, and that can inform them that resist; if God at any time will give them repentance for to know the truth." It becometh not then the Lord's servant to use railing rhymes, but God's word, which is the right weapon to slay sin, vice and all iniquity. The Scripture of God is good to teach and to improve. (2 Tim. iii. and 2 Thess. ii.)   Paul *2 Tim. iii.* *2 Thess. ii.* speaking of Antichrist, saith, " Whom the Lord shall destroy with the Spirit, or breath of his mouth;" that is, with the word of God.   And (2 Cor. x.) " The weapons of our war are not *2 Cor. x.* carnal things, (saith he) but mighty in God to cast down strong holds," and so forth; that is, to destroy high buildings of false doctrine. The word of God is that day whereof Paul speaketh, (1 Cor. iii.) which shall declare all things, and *1 Cor. iii.* that fire which shall try every man's work, and consume false doctrine: with that sword ought men sharply to fight, and not to rail with foolish rhymes.   Let it not offend thee that some walk inordinately; let not the wickedness of Judas cause thee to despise the doctrine of his fellows. No man ought to think that Stephen was a false preacher because that Nicholas, which was

Acts vi. chosen fellow with him (Acts vi.) to minister unto the widows, fell after into great heresies, as histories make mention. Good and evil go always together, one cannot be known without the other.

Antichrist, what it is. Mark this also above all things,—that Antichrist is not an outward thing, that is to say, a man that should suddenly appear with wonders, as our fathers talked of him. No, verily; for Antichrist is a spiritual thing. And is as much to say as against Christ; that is, one that preacheth false doctrine, contrary to Christ. Antichrist was in the Old Testament, and fought with the prophets; he was also in the time of Christ and the apostles, as thou readest in the Epistles of John, and of Paul to the Corinthians and Galatians, and other Epistles. Antichrist is now, and shall, (I doubt not) endure till the world's end. But his nature is (when he is uttered and overcome with the word of God) to go out of the play for a season, and to disguise himself, and then to come in again with a new

Scribes and Pharisees were very Antichrists. name and new raiment. As thou seest how Christ rebuketh the Scribes and the Pharisees in the gospel, (which were very Antichrists,) say-

the pro- perties of Antichrist. ing, "Woe be to you, Pharisees, for ye rob widows' houses; ye pray long prayers under a colour; ye shut up the kingdom of heaven, and suffer them not that would to enter in; ye have taken away the key of knowledge; ye make men break God's commandments with your traditions; ye beguile the people with hypocrisy and such like; Which things all our prelates do, but have yet gotten them new names, and other garments, and are otherwise disguised. There is difference in the names between a pope, a cardinal, a bishop, and so forth, and to say a scribe, a pharisee, a senior, and so forth; but the thing is all one: Even so now, when we have uttered him, he will change himself once more, and turn himself into angel of light. (2 Cor. xi.) Read the place, *2 Cor. 11.* I exhort thee, whatsoever thou art that readest this, and note it well. The Jews look for Christ, *Antichrist* and he is come fifteen hundred years ago, and *hath been* they not aware: we also have looked for Anti- *among us a* christ, and he hath reigned as long, and we not *long time.* aware; and that because either of us looked carnally for him, and not in the places where we ought to have sought. The Jews had found Christ verily if they had sought him in the law and the prophets, whither Christ sendeth them to seek. (John v.) We also had spied out Anti- *John v.* christ long ago if we had looked in the doctrine of Christ and his apostles, where, because the beast seeth himself now to be sought for, he roareth, and seeketh new holes to hide himself in, and changeth himself into a thousand fashions, *Antichrist* with all manner [of] wiliness, falsehood, subtilty, *accounteth* and craft. Because that his excommunications are *it treason* come to light, he maketh it treason unto the *to be acquainted withChrist.*

5

king to be acquainted with Christ. If Christ and
they may not reign together, one hope we have
that Christ shall live ever. The old Antichrists
brought Christ unto Pilate, saying, By our law
he ought to die; and when Pilate bade them
judge him after their law, they answered, It is
not lawful for us to kill any man; which they did
to the intent that they which regarded not the
shame of their false excommunications, should
yet fear to confess Christ, because that the temporal sword had condemned him. They do all
things of a good zeal, they say; they love you
so well, that they had rather burn you, than that
you should have fellowship with Christ. They
are jealous over you amiss, (as saith St. Paul
Gal. iv.) They would divide you from Christ and
his holy Testament, and join you to the Pope,
to believe in his testament and promises. Some
man will ask, peradventure, Why I take the
labour to make this work, inasmuch as they will
burn it, seeing they burnt the gospel? I answer,
In burning the New Testament they did none
other thing than that I looked for, no more shall
they do if they burn me also, if it be God's will
it shall so be.

Nevertheless, in translating the New Testament
I did my duty, and so do I now, and will do as
much more as God hath ordained me to do. And
as I offered that to all men to correct it, whosoever could, even so I do this. Whosoever,
therefore, readeth this, compare it unto the
Scripture. If God's word bear record unto it,

Gal. iv. (margin note)

and thou also feelest in thine heart that it is so, be of good comfort, and give God thanks. If God's word condemn it, then hold it accursed, and so do all other doctrines : as Paul counselleth his Galatians :—Believe not every spirit suddenly, but judge them by the word of God, which is the trial of all doctrine, and lasteth for ever. Amen.

———◆———

THE PARABLE

OF THE

WICKED MAMMON.

———◆———

"There was a certain rich man which had a steward, that was accused **Luke 16.** unto him that he had wasted his goods ; and called him, and said unto him, How is it that I hear this of thee ? Give account of thy stewardship ; for thou mayest be no longer my steward. The steward said within himself, What shall I do, for my master will take away from me my stewardship ? I cannot dig, and to beg I am ashamed. I wot what to do, that when I am put out of my stewardship, they may receive me into their houses. Then called he all his master's debtors, and said unto the first, How much owest thou unto my master ? And he said, An hundred tuns of oil. And he said to him, Take thy bill, and sit down quickly, and write fifty. Then said he to another, What owest thou ? And he said, An hundred quarters of wheat. He said to him, Take thy bill, and write fourscore. And the lord commended the unjust steward, because he had done wisely. For the children of this world are in their kind wiser than the children of light. And I say also unto you, make you friends of the wicked mammon, that when ye shall have need, they may receive you into everlasting habitations." (Luke xvith chapter.)

FORASMUCH as with this, and divers such other texts, many have enforced to draw the people from the true faith, and from putting their trust in the truth of God's promises, and in the merits and deserving of his Christ our Lord ; and have also brought it to pass, (for

7

many false prophets shall arise and deceive many, and
Matt. xxiv. much wickedness must also be, saith Christ; (Matt. xxiv.)
2 Tim. iii. and Paul saith, (2 Tim. iii.) Evil men and deceivers
shall prevail in evil, while they deceive, and are deceived
themselves;) and have taught them to put their trust in
their own merits; and brought them in belief that they
shall be justified in the sight of God by the goodness of
their own works, and have corrupted the pure word of
God, to confirm their Aristotle withal. For though that
the philosophers, and worldly wise men, were enemies
above all enemies to the gospel of God; and though the
worldly wisdom cannot comprehend the wisdom of God,
1 Cor. i. as thou mayest see 1 Cor. i. and ii. And though worldly
and ii. righteousness cannot be obedient unto the righteousness of
Rom. x. God, (Rom. x.) yet whatsoever they read in Aristotle,
that must be first true. And to maintain that, they rend
and tear the Scriptures with their distinctions, and expound them violently, contrary to the meaning of the text,
and to the circumstances that go before and after, and to
a thousand clear and evident texts. Wherefore I have
taken in hand to expound this gospel, and certain other
places of the New Testament; and, (as far forth as God
shall lend me grace,) to bring the Scripture unto the
right sense, and to dig again the wells of Abraham, and
to purge and cleanse them of the earth of worldy wisdom
wherewith these Philistines have stopped them. Which
grace, grant me, God, for the love that he hath unto
his Son, Jesus our Lord, unto the glory of his name.
Amen.

Faith only   THAT faith only before all works and without all merits,
justifieth. but Christ's only, justifieth and setteth us at peace with
God, is proved by Paul in the first chapter to the Romans.
Romans i. I am not ashamed (saith he) of the gospel, that is to say,
of the glad tidings and promises which God hath made,
and sworn to us in Christ. For it (that is to say the gospel)
is the power of God unto salvation to all that believe.

8

And it followeth in the foresaid chapter, the just or righteous must live by faith.

For in the faith which we have in Christ, and in God's promises find we mercy, life, favour and peace. In the law we find death, damnation, and wrath: moreover, the curse and vengeance of God upon us. And it (that is to say the law) is called of Paul (2 Cor. iii.) the ministration of death and damnation. In the law we are proved to be the enemies of God, and that we hate him. For how can we be at peace with God and love him, seeing we are conceived and born under the power of the devil, and are his possession and kingdom, his captives and bondmen, and led at his will, and he holdeth our hearts, so that it is impossible for us to consent to the will of God, much more is it impossible for a man to fulfil the law of his own strength and power, seeing that we are by birth and of nature, the heirs of eternal damnation. As saith Paul, Eph. ii. We (saith he) are by nature the children of wrath, which thing the law doth but utter only, and helpeth us not, yea requireth impossible things of us. The law when it commandeth that thou shalt not lust, giveth thee not power so to do, but damneth thee, because thou canst not so do.

Faith bringeth life.

The law bringeth death. 2 Cor. iii.

Eph ii.

If thou wilt therefore be at peace with God, and love him, thou must turn to the promises of God, and to the gospel, which is called of Paul in the place before rehearsed to the Corinthians, the ministration of righteousness, and of the Spirit. For faith bringeth pardon, and forgiveness freely purchased by Christ's blood, and bringeth also the Spirit, the Spirit looseth the bonds of the devil, and setteth us at liberty. For where the Spirit of the Lord is, there is liberty, saith Paul in the same place to the Corinthians, that is to say, there the heart is free, and hath power to love the will of God, and there the heart mourneth that he cannot love enough. Now is that consent of the heart unto the law of God eternal life, yea, though there be no

The gospel is the ministration of righteousness.

power yet in the members to fulfil it.   Let every man therefore (according to Paul's counsel in the vith chapter to the Ephesians,) arm himself with the armour of God; that is to understand, with God's promises. And above all things (saith he) take unto you the shield of faith, where-with ye may be able to quench all the fiery darts of the wicked, that ye may be able to resist in the evil day of temptation, and namely at the hour of death.

Resist the devil with the shield of faith.

See therefore thou have God's promises in thine heart, and that thou believe them without wavering ; and when temptation ariseth, and the devil layeth the law and thy deeds against thee, answer him with the promises, and turn to God, and confess thyself to him, and say, it is even so or else how could he be merciful ? but remember that he is the God of mercy and of truth, and cannot but fulfil his promises.   Also remember, that his son's blood is stronger than all the sins and wickedness of the whole world, and therewith quiet thyself, and thereunto commit thyself and bless thyself in all temptation, (namely at the hour of death) with that holy candle.   Or else perishest thou, though thou hast a thousand holy candles about thee, a hundred ton of holy water, a ship full of pardons, a cloth-sack full of friar's coats, and all the ceremonies in the world, and all the good works, deservings, and merits of all the men in the world, be they, or were they, never so holy. God's word only lasteth for ever, and that which he hath sworn doth abide, when all other things perish.   So long as thou findest any consent in thine heart unto the law of God, that it is righteous and good, and also displeasure that thou canst not fulfil it, despair not, neither doubt but that God's Spirit is in thee, and that thou art chosen for Christ's sake to the inheritance of eternal life.

Faith is the holy candle wherewith we must bless our-selves at the last hour.

Romans iii.

And again, (Rom. iii.) We suppose that a man is justified through faith, without the deeds of the law.   And likewise (Rom. iv.) we say that faith was reckoned to Abraham for righteousness. Also (Rom. v.) seeing that we are justified through faith, we are at peace with God.   Also (Rom x.)

Romans iv. Faith is ac-counted to us for righ-teousness.

10

with the heart doth a man believe to be made righteous.
Also (Gal. iii.) received ye the Spirit by the deeds of the
law, or by hearing of the faith? Doth he which ministereth the Spirit unto you, and worketh miracles among
you, do it of the deeds of the law, or by hearing of faith?
Even as Abraham believed God, and it was reckoned [to]
him for righteousness. Understand therefore (saith he)
that the children of faith are the children of Abraham.
For the Scripture saw before that God would justify the
heathen or gentiles by faith, and shewed before glad tidings
unto Abraham, In thy seed shall all nations be blessed.
Wherefore they which are of faith are blessed, that is to
wit, made righteous with righteous Abraham. For as
many as are of the deeds of the law, are under curse. For
it is written (saith he) Cursed is every man that continueth
not in all things which are written in the book of the law,
to fulfil them.

Gal. iii.

The children of faith are the children of Abraham.

Also, (Gal. ii.) where he resisted Peter in the face, he
saith, We which are Jews by nation, and not sinners of the
Gentiles, know that a man is not justified by the deeds of
the law, but by the faith of Jesus Christ, and have therefore
believed on Jesus Christ, that we might be justified by the
faith of Christ, and not by the deeds of the law, for by the
deeds of the law shall no flesh be justified. Item, in the
same place he saith, Touching that I now live, I live in the
faith of the son of God, which loved me, and gave himself
for me; I despise not the grace of God, for if righteousness come by the law, then Christ is dead in vain. And
of such like ensamples are all the Epistles of Paul full.
Mark how Paul laboureth with himself to express the exceeding mysteries of faith, in the Epistle to the Ephesians,
and in the Epistle to the Colossians. Of these and many
such like texts, are we sure that the forgiveness of sins
and justifying [are] appropriate unto faith only, without the
adding to of works.

Gal. ii.

Faith only justifieth us.

Take forth also the similitude that Christ maketh, (Mat.
vii.) A good tree bringeth forth good fruit, and a bad tree

Mat. vii.

11

bringeth forth bad fruit.　There seest thou, that the fruit maketh not the tree good, but the tree the fruit; and that the tree must aforehand be good, or be made good, ere it

Mat. xii.　can bring forth good fruit.　As he also saith, (Matt. xii.) Either make the tree good and his fruit good also, either make the tree bad and his fruit bad also.　How can ye speak well while ye yourselves are evil?　So likewise is this true, and nothing more true, that a man before all good works must first be good, and that it is impossible that works should make him good, if he were not good before,

A principle　ere he did good works.　For this is Christ's principle and
taught by　(as we say) a general rule.　How can ye speak well,
Christ.　while ye are evil?　so likewise how can ye do good, while ye are evil?

This is therefore a plain, and a sure conclusion not to be doubted of, that there must be first in the heart of a man before he do any good works, a greater and a more precious thing than all the good works in the world, to reconcile him to God, to bring the love and favour of God to him, to make him love God again, to make him righteous and good in the sight of God, to do away his sin, to deliver him and loose him out of that captivity wherein he was conceived and born, in which he could neither love God, neither the will of God.　Or else how can he work any good work that should please God, if there were not some supernatural goodness in him given of God freely, whereof that good work must spring?　even as a sick man must first be healed or made whole, ere he can do the deeds of an whole man; and as the blind man must first have sight given him ere he can see; and he that hath his feet in fetters, gives, or stocks, must first be loosed, ere he can go, walk or run, and even as they which thou readest of in the gospel, that they were possessed of the devils, could

Faith be-　not laud God till the devils were cast out.
ing joined
with the　That precious thing which must be in the heart, ere a
word of　man can work any good work, is the word of God, which
God, bring-　in the gospel preacheth, profereth, and bringeth unto all
eth forth
good fruit.

12

that repent and believe, the favour of God in Christ. Whosoever heareth the word and believeth it, the same is thereby righteous, and thereby is given him the Spirit of God, which leadeth him unto all that is the will of God, and is loosed from the captivity and bondage of the devil, and his heart is free to love God, and hath lust to do the will of God. Therefore it is called the word of life, the word of grace, the word of health, the word of redemption, the word of forgiveness, and the word of peace ; he that heareth it not, or believeth it not, can by no means be made righteous before God. This confirmeth Peter in the xvth Acts xv. of the Acts, saying that God through faith doth purify the hearts. For of what nature soever the word of God is, of the same nature must the hearts be which believe thereon, and cleave thereunto. Now is the word living, pure, righteous and true, and even so maketh it the hearts of them that believe thereon.

IF it be said that Paul (when he saith in the iiird to the Romans, No flesh shall be, or can be justified by the deeds of the law) meaneth it of the ceremonies or sacrifices, it is a lie, verily. For it followeth immediately,— by the law cometh the knowledge of sin. Now are they not the ceremonies that utter sin, but the law of commandments. In the ivth he saith The law causeth wrath, which cannot be understood of the ceremonies, for they were given to reconcile the people to God again after they had sinned. If, as they say, the ceremonies which were given to purge sin and to reconcile, justify not, neither The law bless but temporally, much more the law of command- cannot jus- ments justifieth not. For that which proveth a man sick, tify us. healeth him not, neither doth the cause of wrath bring to favour, neither can that which damneth save a man. When the mother commandeth her child but even to rock the cradle, it grudgeth, the commandment doth but utter the poison that lay hid, and setteth him at bate [contention] with his mother, and maketh him believe she loveth him not.

13

These commandments also, Thou shalt not covet thy neighbour's house, thou shalt not lust, desire, or wish after thy neighbour's wife, servant, maid, ox, or ass, or whatsoever pertaineth unto thy neighbour, give me not power so to do, but u·ter the poison that is in me and damn me because I cannot so do, and prove that God is wrath with me, seeing that his will and mine are so contrary. Therefore saith

Gal. iii.

Paul, (Gal. iii.) If there had been given such a law that could have given life, then no doubt righteousness had come by the law, but the Scripture concludeth all under sin (saith he) that the promise might be given unto them that believe through the faith that is in Jesus Christ.

Faith in
Christ's
promises
doth justify
us.

The promises, when they are believed, are they that justify, for they bring the Spirit which looseth the heart, giveth lust to the law, and certifieth us unto the good-will of God unto usward. If we submit ourselves unto God and desire him to heal us, he will do it, and will in the mean time (because of the consent of the heart unto the law) count us for full whole, and will no more hate us, but pity us, cherish us, be tender hearted to us, and love us as he doth Christ himself. Christ is our Redeemer, Saviour, peace, atonement and satisfaction, and hath made amends or satisfaction to Godward for all the sin which they that repent (consenting to the law and believing the promises) do, have done, or shall do. So that if through fragility

Christ is
the store-
house of
mercy for
us.

we fall a thousand times in a day, yet if we do repent again, we have alway mercy laid up for us in store in Jesus Christ our Lord.

WHAT shall we say then to those Scriptures which go so sore upon good works? As we read Matt. xxv. I was an hungred, and ye gave me meat, &c. and such like. Which all sound as though we should be justified, and accepted unto the favour of God in Christ through good works. Thiswise answer I, Many there are, which when they hear or read of faith, at once they consent thereunto, and have a certain imagination or opinion of faith, as when

a man telleth a story or a thing done in a strange land, that
pertaineth not to them at all.   Which yet they believe, and
tell as a true thing.   And this imagination or opinion they
call faith.   They think no farther than that faith is a thing *The defini-*
which standeth in their own power to have, as to do other na- *tion of*
tural works which men work; but they feel no manner *true faith.*
[of] working of the Spirit, neither the terrible sentence
of the law, the fearful judgments of God, the horrible
damnation and captivity under Satan.   Therfore as soon
as they have this opinion, or imagination in their hearts,
that saith, Verely this doctrine seemeth true, I believe it is
even so.   Then they think that the right faith is there.
But afterward when they feel in themselves, and also see in
other, that there is none alteration, and that the works
follow not, but that they are altogether even as before, and
abide in their old estate; then think they that faith is not
sufficient, but that it must be some greater thing than faith
that should justify a man.

So fall they away from faith again, and cry, saying, Faith
only justifieth not a man, and maketh him acceptable to
God.   If thou ask them, Wherefore? they answer, See
how many there are that believe, and yet do no more than
they did before.   These are they which Jude in his epis- *Faith that*
tle calleth dreamers which deceive themselves with their *bringeth*
own fantasies.   For what other thing is their imagination *not forth*
which they call faith, than a dreaming of faith, and an *fruit, is but*
opinion of their own imagination wrought without the grace *a dream.*
of God?   These must needs be worse at the latter end
than at the beginning.   These are the old vessels that rent
when new wine is poured into them; (Mat. ix.) that is, they *Mat. ix,*
hear God's word, but hold it not, and therefore wax
worse than they were before.   But the right [faith] springeth
not of man's fantasy, neither is it in any man's power to
obtain it, but is altogether the pure gift of God poured *Faith is the*
into us freely, without all manner [of] doing of us, without *gift of God.*
deserving and merits, yea and without seeking for of us.
And is (as saith Paul in the second to the Ephesians) even *Eph. ii.*

God's gift and grace purchased through Christ. Therefore is it mighty in operation, full of virtue, and ever
working, which also reneweth a man, and begetteth him
afresh, altereth him, changeth him, and turneth him altogether into a new nature and conversation, so that a man
feeleth his heart altogether altered and changed, and far otherwise disposed than before, and hath power to love that
which before he could not but hate, and delighteth in that
which before he abhorred, and hateth that which before he
could not but love. And it setteth the soul at liberty, and
maketh her free to follow the will of God, and doth to the
soul even as health doth unto the body; after that a man is
pined and wasted away with a long soaking disease, the legs
cannot bear him, he cannot lift up his hands to help himself,
his taste is corrupt, sugar is bitter in his mouth, his stomach
abhorreth [meat,] longing after slibbersauce and swash, at
which a whole stomach is ready to cast his gorge. When
health cometh, she changeth and altereth him clean, giveth
him strength in all his members, and lust to do of his own
accord that which before he could not do, neither could
suffer that any man exhorted him to do, and hath now
lust in other things, and his members are free and at
liberty, and have power to do of their own accord all
things, which belong to an whole man to do, which afore
they had no power to do, but were in captivity and
bondage. So likewise in all things doth right faith to the
soul.

The Spi-
rit of God
accompani-
eth faith. The Spirit of God accompanieth faith, and bringeth
with her light, wherewith a man beholdeth himself in the
law of God, and seeth his miserable bondage and captivity, and humbleth himself, and abhorreth himself; she
bringeth God's promises of all good things in Christ. God
worketh with his word, and in his word. And as his word
is preached, faith rooteth herself in the hearts of the elect,
and as faith entereth, and the word of God is believed, the
power of God looseth the heart from the captivity and
bondage under sin, and knitteth and coupleth him to God,

and to the will of God; altereth him, changeth him clean,
fashioneth, and forgeth him anew, giveth him power to
love, and to do that which before was impossible for him
either to love or do, and turneth him unto a new nature,
so that he loveth that which he before hated, and hateth that
which he before loved; and is clean altered, and changed,
and contrary disposed; and is knit and coupled fast to
God's will, and naturally bringeth forth good works, that
is to say, that which God commandeth to do, and not
things of his own imagination.   And that doth he of his
own accord, as a tree bringeth forth fruit of her own accord.
And as thou needest not to bid a tree to bring forth fruit,
so is there no law put unto him that believeth, and is justified through faith (as saith Paul in the first Epistle to
Timothy, the first chapter).   Neither is it needful, for
the law of God is written and graved in his heart, and his
pleasure is therein.   And as without commandment, but
even of his own nature, he eateth, drinketh, seeth, heareth,
talketh, and goeth, even so of his own nature, without co-
action or compulsion of the law, bringeth he forth good
works.   And as a whole man, when he is athirst, tarrieth
but for drink, and when he hungreth abideth but for meat,
and then drinketh and eateth naturally; even so is the
faithful ever athirst, and an hungred after the will of God,
and tarrieth but for occasion.   And whensoever an occasion is given, he worketh naturally the will of God: for
this blessing is given to all them that trust in Christ's
blood, that they thirst and hunger to do God's will.   He
that hath not this faith, is but an unprofitable babler of
faith and works, and wotteth neither what he bableth, nor
what he meaneth, or whereunto his words pertain: for he
feeleth not the power of faith, ncr the working of the
Spirit in his heart, but interpreteth the Scriptures, which
speak of faith and works, after his own blind reason and
foolish fantasies, and not of any feeling that he hath in his
heart;—as a man rehearseth a tale of another man's
mouth, and wotteth not whether it be so or no, as he saith,

Faith of herself bringeth forth good fruits, that is, good works.

True faith is not without good works.

17

nor hath any experience of the thing itself. Now doth the Scripture ascribe both faith and works, not to us, but to God only, to whom they belong only, and to whom they are appropriate, whose gift they are, and the proper work of his Spirit.

Is it not a froward and perverse blindness, to teach how a man can do nothing of his own self, and yet presumptuously take upon them the greatest and highest work of God, even to make faith in themselves of their own power, and of their own false imagination and thoughts? Therefore, I say, we must despair of ourselves, and pray God (as Christ's apostles did) to give us faith, and to encrease our faith. When we have that, we need no other thing more. For she bringeth the Spirit with her, and he not only teacheth us all things, but worketh them also mightily in us, and carrieth us through adversity, persecution, death, and hell, unto heaven and everlasting life.

MARK diligently, therefore, seeing we are come to answer. The Scripture, (because of such dreams and feigned faith's sake) useth such manner of speakings of works, not that a man should thereby be made good to God-ward, or justified; but to declare unto other, and to take of other the difference between false feigned faith, and right faith. For where right faith is, there bringeth she forth good works; if there follow not good works, it is (no doubt) but a dream and an opinion or feigned faith.

Wherefore look, as the fruit maketh not the tree good, but declareth and testifieth outwardly that the tree is good, (as Christ saith) Every tree is known by his fruit; even so shall ye know the right faith by her fruit.

Take for an ensample Mary that anointed Christ's feet. (Luke vii.) When Simon which had Christ to his house had condemned her, Christ defended her, and justified her, saying, Simon, I have a certain thing to say unto thee, and he said, Master, say on. There was a certain lender which had two debtors, the one owed five hundred pence, and the other fifty. When they had nothing to pay, he forgave both. Which of them, tell me, will love him most? Simon answered and said, I suppose that he to whom he forgave most. And he said to him, Thou hast truly judged. And he turned him to the woman, and said unto Simon, Seest thou this woman? I entered into thine house, and thou gavest me no water to my feet; but she hath washed my feet with tears, and wiped them with the hairs of her head. Thou gavest me no kiss, but she, since the time I came in, hath not ceased to kiss my feet. My head with oil thou hast not anointed. And she hath anointed my feet with costly and precious ointment. Wherefore I say unto thee, many sins are forgiven her, for she loveth much. To whom less is forgiven, the same doth love less, &c. Hereby, see we, that deeds and works are but outward signs of the inward grace of the bounteous and plenteous mercy of God, freely received without all merits of deeds, yea, and before all deeds. Christ teacheth to know the inward faith and love, by the outward deeds. Deeds are the fruits of love, and love is the fruit of faith. Love, and also the deeds, are great or small, according to the proportion of faith. Where faith is mighty and strong, there is love fervent, and deeds plenteous, and done with exceeding meekness: where faith is weak, there is love cold, and the deeds few, and seldom bear flowers and blossoms in winter.

The fruits of faith.

Simon believed, and had faith yet but weakly, and according to the proportion of his faith loved coldly, and had deeds thereafter: he had Christ unto a simple and bare feast only, and received him not with any great humanity. But Mary had a strong faith, and therefore burning love, and honourable deeds, done with exceeding profound and deep meekness. On the one side she saw herself clearly in the law, both in what danger she was in, and her cruel bondage under sin, her horrible damnation, and also the fearful sentence and judgment of God upon sinners. On the other side she heard the gospel of Christ preached, and in the

A difference between true faith and feigned faith.

19

promises she saw with eagles' eyes the exceeding abundant mercy of God that passeth all utterance of speech, which is set forth in Christ for all meek sinners which knowledge their sins; and she believed the word of God mightily, and glorified God over his mercy and truth; and being overcome and overwhelmed with the unspeakable, yea, and incomprehensible abundant riches of the kindness of God, did inflame and burn in love; yea, was so swollen in love, that she could not abide, nor hold, but must break out; and was so drunk in love that she regarded nothing, but even to utter the fervent and burning love of her heart only; she had no respect to herself, though she was never so great and notable a sinner; neither to the curious hypocrisy of the Pharisees, which ever disdain weak sinners; neither the costliness of her ointment; but with all humbleness did run unto his feet; washed them with the tears of her eyes, and wiped them with the hairs of her head, and anointed them with her precious ointment; yea, and would no doubt have run into the ground under his feet, to have uttered her love toward him; yea would have descended down into hell, if it had been possible. Even as Paul in the ixth chapter of his Epistle to the Romans was drunk in love, and over-

Rom. ix. whelmed with the plenteousness of the infinite mercy of God, (which he had received in Christ unsought for) wished himself banished from Christ and damned, to save the Jews, if it might have been. For as a man feeleth God in himself, so is he to his neighbour.

Mark another thing also. We, for the most part, because of our grossness in all our knowledge, proceed from that which is last and hindmost, unto that which is first; beginning at the latter end, disputing and making our arguments backward. We begin at the effect, and work and proceed unto the natural cause. As for an ensample: we first see the moon dark, and then search the cause, and find that the putting of the earth between the sun and the moon is the natural cause

Backward of the darkness, and that the earth stoppeth the light. Then
disputa-
tions. dispute we backward, saying, the moon is darkened, there-

fore is the earth directly between the sun and moon. Now yet is not the darkness of the moon the natural cause that the earth is between the sun and the moon, but the effect thereof, and cause declarative, declaring and leading us unto the knowledge, how that the earth is between the sun and the moon directly, and causeth the darkness, stopping the light of the sun from the moon. And contrarywise, the being of the earth directly between the sun and the moon is the natural cause of the darkness. Likewise he hath a son, therefore is he a father, and yet the son is not cause of the father, but contrarywise. Notwithstanding, the son is the cause declarative, whereby we know that the other is a father. After the same manner here, many sins are forgiven her, for she loveth much, thou mayest not understand by the word for, that love is the natural cause of the forgiving of sins, but declareth it only; and contrariwise, the forgiveness of sins is the natural cause of love.

The works declare love. And love declareth that there is some benefit and kindness shewed, or else would there be no love. Why worketh one and another not? or one more than another? because that one loveth and the other not, or that the one loveth more than the other. Why loveth one and another not, or one more than another? because that one feeleth the exceeding love of God in his heart and another not, or that one feeleth it more than another. Scripture speaketh after the most gross manner. Be diligent therefore that thou be not deceived, with curiousness, for men of no small reputation have been deceived with their own sophistry.

The kindness of God moveth us to loveGod.

HEREBY now seest thou, that there is great difference between being righteous and good in a man's self, and declaring and uttering righteousness and goodness. The faith only maketh a man safe, good, righteous, and the friend of God, yea, and the son and the heir of God, and of all his goodness, and possesseth us with the Spirit of God. The work declareth the self faith and goodness. Now useth the Scripture the common manner of speaking,

Faith only maketh us the sons and heirs of God.

Faith pos-
sesseth the
Spirit of
God.
Works de-
clare faith
and God's
goodness.

and the very same that is among the people. As when a father saith to his child, Go, and be loving, merciful, and good
to such or such a poor man, he biddeth him not therewith
to be made merciful, kind, and good, but to testify and
declare the goodness that is in him already, with the outward deed, that it may break out to the profit of other, and
that other may feel it which have need thereof.

After the same manner shalt thou interpret the Scriptures
which make mention of works: that God thereby will that
we show forth that goodness which we have received by
faith, and let it break forth and come to the profit of other,
that the false faith may be known and weeded out by the
roots. For God giveth no man his grace that he should let
it lay still and do no good withal, but that he should encrease it and multiply it with lending it to others, and with
open declaring of it with the outward works, provoke and
draw others to God. As Christ saith in Matthew the vth.
chapter, Let your light so shine in the sight of men, that they
may see your good works, and glorify your Father which is
in heaven. Or else where it is a treasure digged in the
ground, and hid wisdom, in which what profit is there?

God's grace
is to be ex-
ercised in
us.

Moreover therewith the goodness, favour, and gifts of
God which are in thee, not only shall be known unto other,
but also unto thine own self, and thou shalt be sure that thy
faith is right, and that the true Spirit of God is in thee, and
that thou art called and chosen of God unto eternal life,
and loosed from the bonds of Satan, whose captive thou
wast; as Peter exhorteth in the First of his Second Epistle,
through good works to make our calling and election
(wherewith we are called and chosen of God) sure. For
how dare a man presume to think that his faith is right,
and that God's favour is on him, and that God's Spirit is
in him, when he feeleth not the working of the Spirit, neither himself disposed to any godly thing? Thou canst never know or be sure of thy faith but by the works, if works
follow not, yea, and that of love, without loooking after any
reward, thou mayest be sure that thy faith is but a dream,

Where true
faith is,
good works
follow.

and not right, and even the same that James called in his
Epistle, the second chapter, dead faith and not justifying.

Abraham through works, (Genesis xxiind) was sure of his   Gen. xxii.
faith to be right, and that the true fear of God was in him,
when he had offered his son, as the Scripture saith, Now
know I that thou fearest God, that is to say, now is it
open and manifest that thou fearest God, inasmuch as thou
hast not spared thy only son for my sake.

So now by this abide sure and fast, that a man inwardly
in the heart and before God, is righteous and good through
faith only, before all works: notwithstanding, yet outwardly and openly before the people, yea, and before himself, is he righteous through the work, that is, he knoweth and is sure through the outward work that he is a
true believer, and in the favour of God, and righteous and
good through the mercy of God: that thou mayest call the
one an open and an outward righteousness, and the other,   The out-
an inward righteousness of the heart; so yet, that thou un-   ward righ-
derstand by the outward righteousness, no other thing save   teousness
the fruit that followeth, and a declaring of the inward   and the in-
                                                              ward righ-
justifying and righteousness of the heart, and not that it   teousness
maketh a man righteous before God, but that he must be first what they
righteous before him in the heart; even as thou mayest call the are.
fruit of the tree the outward goodness of the tree, which followeth and uttereth the inward natural goodness of the tree.

This meaneth James in his Epistle, where he saith, Faith
without works is dead, that is, if works follow not, it is a
sure and an evident sign that there is no faith in the heart, but
a dead imagination and dream, which they falsely call faith.

Of the same wise is this saying of Christ to be understood: Make you friends of the unrighteous mammon, that is,   Outward
shew your faith openly and what ye are within in the heart,   works de-
                                                               clare where
with outward giving and bestowing your goods on the poor,   true faith
that ye may obtain friends; that is, that the poor on whom   is.
thou hast showed mercy may at the day of judgment, testify and witness of thy good works. That thy faith and what

thou wast within thy heart before God, may there appear by thy fruits openly to all men.   For unto the right believing shall all things be comfortable, and unto consolation, at that terrible day: and contrariwise unto the unbelieving, all things shall be unto desperation and confusion, and every man shall be judged openly and outwardly, in the presence of all men, according to their deeds and works. So that not without a cause thou mayest call them thy friends which testify at that day of thee, that thou livedst as a true and a right christian man, and followedst the steps of Christ in shewing mercy, as no doubt he doth which feeleth God merciful in his heart.   And by the works is the faith known, that it was right and perfect.   For the outward works can never please God, nor make friend, except they spring of faith.   Forasmuch as Christ himself (Matt. vi. and vii.) disalloweth and casteth away the works of the Pharisees, yea, prophesying and working of miracles and casting out of devils, which we count and esteem for very excellent virtues, yet make they no friends with their works, while their hearts are false and impure, and their eye double. Now without faith is no heart true or eye single, so that we are compelled to confess that the works make not a man righteous or good, but that the heart must first be righteous and good, ere any good work proceed thence.

SECONDARILY, all good works must be done free with a single eye, without respect of any thing, and that no profit be sought thereby.

That commandeth Christ, where he saith, (Mat. x.) Freely have ye received, freely give again.   For look, as Christ with all his works did not deserve heaven, for that was his already, but did us service therewith, and neither looked, nor sought his own profit, but our profit, and the honour of God the Father only ; even so we, with all our works, may not seek our own profit neither in this world nor in heaven, but must, and ought, freely to work to honour God withal, and without all manner [of] respect, seek our

(marginal notes:)

Good works are witnesses for us before God.

Matt. vi. and vii.

Matt. x.

We must of duty do good works without hope of reward.

24

neighbour's profit, and do him service. That meaneth
Paul (Phil. ii.) saying, Be minded as Christ was, which
being in the shape of God, equal unto God, and even very
God, laid that apart, that is to say hid it, and took on him
the form and fashion of a servant. That is, as concerning
himself he had enough, that he was full and had all plen- •
teousness of the Godhead, and in all his works sought our
profit, and became our servant.

The cause is: forasmuch as faith justifieth and putteth
away sin in the sight of God, bringeth life, health, and the
favour of God, maketh us the heirs of God, poureth the
Spirit of God into our souls, and filleth us with all godly
fulness in Christ; it were too great a shame, rebuke and
wrong unto the faith, yea to Christ's blood, if a man would
work any thing to purchase that wherewith faith hath en-
dued him already, and God hath given him freely. Even
as Christ had done rebuke and shame unto himself, if he
would have done good works, and wrought to have been
made thereby God's son and heir over all, which thing he
was already. Now doth faith make us the sons or children
of God. (John i.) He gave them might or power to be
the sons of God, in that they believed on his name.. If
we be sons, so are we also heirs. (Rom. viii.. and Gal.. iv.)
How can or ought we then to work for to purchase that
inheritance withal, whereof we are heirs already by faith?

What shall we say then to those Scriptures, which sound
as though a man should do good works, and live well for
heaven's sake or eternal reward? As these are, Make
you friends of the unrighteous mammon.. And (Mat.. vii.)
Gather you treasures together in heaven.. Also (Mat.
xix.) If thou wilt enter into life, keep the commandments:
and such like.. This say I, that they which understand
not, neither feel in their hearts what faith meaneth, talk
and think of the reward,. even as they do of the work;
neither suppose they that a man ought to work, but in a
respect to the reward. · For they imagine, that it is in the
kingdom of Christ, as it is in the world among men, that

Marginal notes:
Faith mak-
eth us the
sons and
children of
God.
Rom. viii.
Gal. iv.

Mat. vii.

Mat. xix.

They that
seek hea-
ven for
their works
are such as
understand
not the
treasures of
Christ.

they must deserve heaven with their good works. Howbeit their thoughts are but dreams and false imaginations. Of these men speaketh Malachi (chap. i.) Who is it among you that shutteth a door for my pleasure for nought, that is without respect of reward? These are servants that seek gains and vantage, hirelings and day labourers, which here on earth receive their rewards, as the Pharisees with their prayers and fastings. (Mat. v.)

Mat. v.

But on this wise goeth it with heaven, with everlasting life and eternal reward: likewise as good works naturally follow faith (as it is above rehearsed) so that thou needest not to command a true believer to work, or to compel him with any law, for it is unpossible that he should not work; he tarrieth but for an occasion; he is ever disposed of himself, thou needest but to put him in remembrance, and that to know the false faith from the true. Even so naturally doth eternal life follow faith and good living, without seeking for, and is impossible that it should not come, though no man thought thereon. Yet is it rehearsed in the Scripture, alleged and promised to know the difference between a false believer and a true believer, and that every man may know what followeth good living naturally and of itself, without taking thought for it.

As good
works na-
turally fol-
low faith,
so eternal
life follow-
eth faith
and good
living.

As good
works fol-
low faith,
so hell fol-
loweth evil
works.

Take a gross ensample: hell, that is, everlasting death, is threatened unto sinners, and yet followeth it sin naturally without seeking for. For no man doth evil to be damned therefore, but had rather avoid it. Yet there the one followeth the other naturally, and though no man told or warned him of it, yet should the sinner find it and feel it. Nevertheless it is therefore threatened, that men may know what followeth evil living. Now then as after evil living followeth his reward unsought for, even so after good living followeth his reward naturally unsought for, or unthought upon. Even as when thou drinkest wine, be it good or bad, the taste followeth of itself, though thou therefore drink it not. Yet testifieth the Scripture, and it is true, that we are by inheritance heirs of damnation; and that

26

ere we be born, we are vessels of the wrath of God, and full of that poison whence naturally all sins spring; and wherewith we cannot but sin, which thing the deeds that follow (when we behold ourselves in the glass of the law of God) do declare and utter, kill our consciences, and show us what we were and wist not of it, and certifieth us that we are heirs of damnation. For if we were of God we should cleave to God, and lust after the will of God. But now our deeds compared to the law declare the contrary, and by our deeds we see ourselves, both what we be and what our end shall be.

Of ourselves we are the vessels of the wrath of God, and the heirs of damnation.

So now thou seest that life eternal and all good things are promised unto faith and belief; so that he that believeth on Christ shall be safe. Christ's blood hath purchased life for us, and hath made us the heirs of God; so that heaven cometh by Christ's blood. If thou wouldst obtain heaven with the merits and deservings of thine own works, so didst thou wrong, yea, and shamedst the blood of Christ, and unto thee were Christ dead in vain. Now is the true believer heir of God by Christ's deservings, yea, and in Christ was predestinate and ordained unto eternal life before the world began. And when the gospel is preached unto us, we believe the mercy of God, and in believing we receive the Spirit of God, which is the earnest of eternal life, and we are in eternal life already, and feel already in our hearts the sweetness thereof, and are overcome with the kindness of God and Christ, and therefore love the will of God, and of love are ready to work freely, and not to obtain that which is given us freely, and whereof we are heirs already.

To believe Christ is salvation.

To seek heaven by good works were to derogate the dignity of the blood of Christ.

Now when Christ saith, Make you friends of unrighteous Mammon: Gather you treasure together in heaven, and such like: thou seest that the meaning and intent is no other but that thou shouldst do good, and so will it follow of itself naturally, without seeking and taking of thought, that thou shalt find friends and treasure in heaven, and receive a reward. So let thine eye be single, and look

unto good living only, and take no thought for the reward,
but be content. Forasmuch as thou knowest and art sure
that the reward and all things contained in God's promises
follow good living naturally; and thy good works do but
testify only, and certify thee that the Spirit of God is in
thee, whom thou hast received in earnest of God's truth;

All that is good is purchased for us by Christ.

and that thou art heir of all the goodness of God, and that
all good things are thine already, purchased by Christ's blood,
and laid up in store against that day, when every man shall
receive according to his deeds, that is according as his
deeds declare and testify, what he is or was. For they
that look unto the reward, are slow, false, subtle and crafty
workers, and love the reward more than the work, yea,
hate the labour, yea, hate God which commandeth the
labour, and are weary both of the commandment, and
also of the Commander, and work with tediousness. But
he that worketh of pure love, without seeking of reward,
worketh truly.

Saints cannot help us into heaven.

Thirdly, that not the saints, but God only receiveth us
into eternal tabernacles, is so plain and evident, that it
needeth not to declare or prove it. How shall the saints
receive us into heaven, when every man hath need for himself that God only receive him to heaven, and every man
hath scarce for himself? As it appeareth by the five wise

Mat. xxv.

virgins, (Mat. xxv.) which would not give of their oil unto
the unwise virgins. And Peter saith in the ivth of his

1 Pet. iv.

first Epistle, that the righteous is with difficulty saved.
So seest thou the saying of Christ, Make you friends, and
so forth, that they may receive you into everlasting tabernacles, pertaineth not unto the saints which are in heaven,
but is spoken of the poor and needy which are here present
with us on earth: as though he should say, What, buildest
thou churches, foundest abbeys, chauntries and colleges,
in the honour of saints, to my Mother, St. Peter, Paul, and
saints that be dead, to make of them thy friends? They
need it not, yea, they are not thy friends, but theirs which
lived then when they did, of whom they were holpen.

Thy friends are the poor, which are now in thy time, and live with thee ; thy poor neighbours which need thy help and succour. Them make thy friends with thy unrighteous mammon, that they may testify of thy faith, and thou mayest know and feel that thy faith is right and not feigned.

How we may make friends of the wicked mammon.

UNTO the second, such receiving into everlasting habitations is not to be understood that men shall do it. For many, to whom we shew mercy and do good, shall not come there ; neither skilleth it so we meekly and lovingly do our duty, yea, it is a sign of strong faith and fervent love, if we do well to the evil, and study to draw them to Christ in all that lieth in us. But the poor give us an occasion to exercise our faith, and the deeds make us feel our faith, and certify us and make us sure that we are safe, and are escaped and translated from death unto life, and that we are delivered and redeemed from the captivity and bondage of Satan, and brought into the liberty of the sons of God, in that we feel lust and strength ·in our heart to work the will of God. And at that day shall our deeds appear and comfort our hearts, witness our faith and trust, which we now have in Christ, which faith shall then keep us from shame, as it is written, None that believeth in him shall be ashamed, (Rom. ix.) So that good works help our faith, and make us sure in our consciences, and make us feel the mercy of God. Notwithstanding, heaven, everlasting life, joy eternal, faith, the favour of God, the Spirit of God, lust and strength unto the will of God, are given us freely of the bounteous and plenteous riches of God, purchased by Christ, without our deservings, that no man should rejoice but in the Lord only.

To do good to such as are evil, is commendable.

Rom. ix.

All our righteousness cometh freely from Christ.

FOR a farther understanding of this gospel, here may be made three questions, What mammon is, Why it is called unrighteous, and after what manner Christ biddeth us counterfeit and follow the unjust and wicked steward, which with his Lord's damage provided for his own profit and vantage, which thing no doubt is unrighteous and sin ?

First, *mammon* is an Hebrew word, and signifies riches
or temporal goods, and namely, all superfluity, and all that
is above necessity, and that which is required unto our ne-
cessary uses, wherewith a man may help another without
undoing or hurting himself; for Hamon, in the Hebrew
speech, signifies a multitude or abundance, or many, and
there hence cometh mahamon, or mammon, abundance or
plenteousness of good or riches.

Secondarily, it is called unrighteous mammon, not because it is got unrighteously, or with usury, for of unrighteous
gotten goods can no man do good works, but ought to restore them home again. As it is said (Isaiah lxi.) I am a
God that hateth offering that cometh of robbery; and Solo-
mon (Prov. iii.) saith, Honour the Lord of thine own good.
But therefore it is called unrighteous, because it is in unrighteous use. As Paul speaketh unto the Ephesians vth.
how that The days are evil though that God hath made
them, and they are a good work of God's making. Howbeit they are yet called evil, because that evil men use them
amiss, and much sin, occasions of evil, peril of souls are
wrought in them. Even so are riches called evil because
that evil men bestow them amiss and misuse them. For
where riches are there goeth it after the common proverb,
He that hath money hath what him listeth. And they cause
fighting, stealing, laying await, lying, flattering, and all un-
happiness against a man's neighbour. For all men hold on
riches' part.

But singularly before God is it called unrighteous mammon, because it is not bestowed and ministered unto our
neighbour's need. For if my neighbour need and I give him
not, neither depart liberally with him of that which I have,
then withhold I from him unrighteously that which is his
own. For as much as I am bounden to help him by the law
of nature, which is Whatsoever thou wouldest that another
did to thee, that do thou also to him; and Christ (Matt. v.)
Give to every man that desireth thee; and John in his first
Epistle, If a man have this world's good and see his brother

Isaiah lxi.

Prov. iii.

Ephes. v.

The days
are called
evil, be-
cause evil
men use
them.

We are
bound by
the law of
nature to
help our
needy
neighbour.

need, how is the love of God in him? And this unrighteousness in our mammon see very few men: because it is spiritual, and in those goods which are gotten most truly and justly, which beguile men. For they suppose they do no man wrong in keeping them, in that they got them not with stealing, robbing, oppression, and usury, neither hurt any man now with them.

Thirdly, many have busied themselves in studying what, or who, this unrighteous steward is, because that Christ so praiseth him. But shortly and plainly this is the answer. That Christ praiseth not the unrighteous steward, neither setteth him forth to us to counterfeit because of his unrighteousness, but because of his wisdom only, in that he, with unright, so wisely provided for himself. As if I would provoke another to pray or study, say, The thieves watch all night to rob and steal, why canst not thou watch to pray and to study? here praise not I the thief and murderer for their evil doing, but for their wisdom, that they so wisely and diligently wait on their unrighteousness. Likewise when I say miss women tire themselves with gold and silk to please their lovers: what wilt not thou garnish thy soul with faith to please Christ? here praise I not whoredom, but the diligence which the whore misuseth.

The unrighteous steward, who it is.

On this wise Paul also (Rom. v.) likeneth Adam and Christ together, saying that Adam was a figure of Christ. And yet of Adam have we but pure sin, and of Christ grace only, which are out of measure contrary. But the similitude or likeness standeth in the original birth, and not in the virtue and vice of the birth. So that as Adam is father of all sin, so is Christ father of all righteousness: and as all sinners spring of Adam, even so all righteous men and women spring of Christ. After the same manner is here the unrighteous steward an ensample unto us, in his wisdom and diligence only, in that he provided so wisely for himself, that we with righteousness should be as diligent to provide for our souls as he with unrighteousness provided for his body.

Christ is the Father of all righteousness.

Likewise mayest thou solve all other texts which sound as though it were between us and God, as it is in the world, where the reward is more looked upon than the labour; yea, where men hate the labour, and work falsely with the body and not with the heart, and no longer than they are looked upon, that the labour may appear outward only.

Matt. v.

WHEN Christ saith (Matt. v.) Blessed are ye when they rail on you, and persecute you, and say all manner [of] evil sayings against you, and yet lie, and that for my sake, rejoice and be glad, for your reward is great in heaven. Thou mayest not imagine that our deeds deserve the joy and glory that shall be given unto us, for then Paul saith (Rom, xi.) Favour were not favour, I cannot receive it of favour and of the bounties of God freely, and by deserving of deeds also. But believe as the gospel, glad tidings and promises of God say unto thee, that for Christ's blood sake only, through faith, God is at one with thee, and thou received to mercy, and art become the son of God and heir annexed with Christ, of all the goodness of God, the earnest whereof is the Spirit of God poured into our hearts. Of which things the deeds are witnesses, and certify our consciences that our faith is unfeigned, and that the right Spirit of God is in us. For if I patiently suffer adversity and tribulation for conscience of God only, that is to say, because I know God and testify the truth, then am I sure that God hath chosen me in Christ and for Christ's sake, and hath put in me his Spirit as an earnest of his promises, whose working I feel in mine heart, the deeds bearing witness unto the same. Now is it Christ's blood only that deserved all the promises of God, and that which I suffer and do, is partly the curing, healing, and mortifying of my members, and killing of that original poison, wherewith I was conceived and born, that I might be altogether like Christ, and partly the doing of my duty to my neighbour, whose debtor I am of all that I have received of God; to draw him to Christ with all suffering, with all patience, and

ForChrist's blood sake, only through faith, God is at one with us.

even with shedding my blood for him, not as an offering or merit for his sins, but as an ensample to provoke him. Christ's blood only putteth away all the sin that ever was, is, or shall be, from them that are elect and repent, believing the gospel, that is to say, God's promises in Christ.

Christ's blood only putteth away all sin.

AGAIN in the same vth chapter, Love your enemies, bless them that curse you, do well to them that hate you and persecute you, that ye may be sons of your father which is in heaven: for he maketh his sun shine upon evil, and on good, and sendeth his rain upon just and unjust. Not that our works make us the sons of God, but testify only, and certify our consciences, that we are the sons of God, and that God hath chosen us, and washed us in Christ's blood, and hath put his Spirit in us. And it followeth, If ye love them that love you, what reward have ye? do not the Publicans even the same? and if ye shall have favour to your friends only, what singular thing do ye? do not the Publicans even the same? Ye shall be perfect therefore, as your Father which is in heaven is perfect. That is to say, if that ye do nothing but that the world doth, and they which have the spirit of the world, whereby shall ye know that ye are the sons of God, and beloved of God more than the world? But, and if ye counterfeit, and follow God in well doing, then no doubt it is a sign that the Spirit of God is in you, and also the favour of God, which is not in the world, and that ye are inheritors of all the promises of God, and elect unto the fellowship of the blood of Christ.

We must follow Christ in well doing.

ALSO (Matt. vi.) Take heed to your alms, that ye do it not in the sight of men, to the intent that ye would be seen of them, or else have ye no reward with your Father which is in heaven. Neither cause a trumpet to be blown afore thee when thou doest thine alms, as the hypocrites

Matt. vi.

We may not do good works to be praised of the world.

do in the synagogues, and in the streets, to be glorified of the world. But when thou doest thine alms, let not thy left hand know what thy right hand doth; that thy alms may be in secret, and thy Father which seeth in secret shall reward thee openly. This putteth us in remembrance of our duty, and sheweth what followeth good works; not that works deserve it, but that the reward is laid up for us in store, and we thereunto elect through Christ's blood, which the works testify: for, if we be worldly minded, and do our works as the world doth, how shall we know that God hath chosen us out of the world? But and if we work freely, without all manner [of] worldly respect,

We must do to our neighbour as God is to us.

to shew mercy, and to do our duty to our neighbour, and to be unto him as God is to us, then are we sure that the favour and mercy of God is upon us, and that we shall enjoy all the good promises of God through Christ, which hath made us heirs thereof.

Hypocrites seek to be praised of men.

ALSO, in the same chapter it followeth, When thou prayest, be not as the hypocrites, which love to stand and pray in the synagogues, and in the corners of the streets, for to be seen of men. But when thou prayest, enter into thy chamber, and shut thy door to, and pray to thy Father which is in secret, and thy Father which seeth in secret, shall reward thee openly. And likewise, when we fast (teacheth Christ in the same place) that we should behave ourselves that it appear not unto men how that we fast, but unto our Father which is in secret, and our Father which seeth in secret, shall reward us openly. These two texts do but declare what followeth good works, for eternal life cometh not by the deserving of works, but is, (saith Paul, in the vith to

Rom. vi.

the Romans) the gift of God through Jesus Christ. Neither do our works justify us. For except we were justified

Faith only justifieth us and no good works can be done without faith.

by faith which is our righteousness, and had the Spirit of God in us, to teach us, we could do no good work freely, without respect of some profit, either in this world, or in the world to come; neither could we have spiritual

34

joy in our hearts in time of affliction, and mortifying of
the flesh.

Good works are called the fruits of the Spirit, (Gal. v.)
for the Spirit worketh them in us, and sometime fruits of
righteousness, as in the second Epistle to the Corinthians
and ixth chapter.   Before all works therefore, we must have
a righteousness within in the heart, the mother of all works,
and from whence they spring.   The righteousness of the
Scribes and Pharisees, and of them that have the spirit of
this world, is the glorious shew and outward shining of
works.   But Christ saith to us (Mat. v.) Except your
righteousness exceed the righteousness of the Scribes and
Pharisees ye cannot enter into the kingdom of heaven.   It
is righteousness in the world if a man kill not.   But a christian perceiveth righteousness if he love his enemy, even
when he suffereth persecution and torment of him, and the
pains of death, and mourneth more for his adversary's
blindness than for his own pain, and prayeth God to open
his eyes and to forgive him his sins, as did Stephen in the
Acts of the Apostles the viith chapter, and Christ, Luke
xxiii.

A Christian considereth himself in the law of God,
and there putteth off him all manner [of] righteousness.
For the law suffereth no merits, no deservings, no righteousness, neither any man to be justified in the sight of
God.   The law is spiritual and requireth the heart and
commandments to be fulfilled with such love and obedience
as was in Christ.   If any fulfil all that is the will of God
with such love and obedience, the same may be bold to
sell pardons of his merits, and else not.

A Christian therefore when he beholdeth himself in the
law, putteth off all manner [of] righteousness, deservings
and merits, and meekly and unfeignedly knowledgeth his
sin and misery, his captivity and bondage in the flesh, his
trespass and guilt, and is thereby blessed with the poor in
spirit. (Mat. chap. v.)   Then he mourneth in his heart,
because he is in such bondage that he cannot do the will of

Good works are the fruits of faith.

True righteousness what it is.

Acts vii.

Luke xxiii.

35

God, and is an hungred and athirst after righteousness. For righteousness (I mean) which springeth out of Christ's blood, for strength to do the will of God. And turneth himself to the promises of God, and desireth him for his great mercy and truth, and for the blood of his son Christ to fulfil his promises and to give him strength. And thus his Spirit ever prayeth within him. He fasteth also not one day for a week, or a lent for an whole year, but professeth in his heart a perpetual soberness, to tame the flesh, and to subdue the body to the Spirit, until he wax strong in the Spirit, and grow ripe into a full righteousness after the fulness of Christ. And because this fulness happeneth not till the body be slain by death, a christian is ever a sinner in the law, and therefore fasteth and prayeth to God in the Spirit, the world seeing it not. Yet in the promises he is ever righteous through faith in Christ, and is sure that he is heir of all God's promises, the Spirit which he hath received in earnest, bearing him witness, his heart also, and his deeds testifying the same.

Mark this then: To see inwardly that the law of God is so spiritual, that no flesh can fulfil it. And then for to mourn and sorrow and to desire, yea to hunger and thirst after strength to do the will of God from the ground of the heart, and, (notwithstanding all the subtilty of the devil, weakness and feebleness of the flesh, and wondering of the world,) to cleave yet to the promises of God, and to believe that for Christ's blood sake thou art received to the inheritance of eternal life, is a wonderful thing, and a thing that the world knoweth not of; but whosoever feeleth that, though he fall a thousand times in a day, doth yet rise again a thousand times, and is sure that the mercy of God is upon him.

IF ye forgive other men their trespasses, your heavenly Father shall forgive you yours. (Mat. chap. vi.) If I forgive, God shall forgive me, not for my deeds' sake, but for his promises' sake, for his mercy and truth, and for the

Side notes:

True righteousness springeth out of Christ's blood.

True fasting what it is.

No flesh can fulfil the law.

We cannot deserve forgiveness of God.

blood of his Son, Christ our Lord. And my forgiving
certifieth my spirit that God shall forgive me, yea that he
hath forgiven me already. For if I consent to the will of
God in my heart, though through infirmity and weakness
I cannot do the will of God at all times; moreover though
I cannot do the will of God so purely as the law requireth
it of me, yet if I see my fault and meekly knowledge my
sin, weeping in mine heart, because I cannot do the will of
God; and thirst after strength, I am sure that the Spirit of
God is in me, and his favour upon me. For the world
lusteth not to do the will of God, neither sorroweth because
he cannot, though he sorrow some time for fear of the pain
that he believeth shall follow. He that hath the spirit of
this world cannot forgive without amends making, or a
greater vantage. If I forgive now how cometh it? Verily
because I feel the mercy of God in me. For as a man
feeleth God to himself, so is he to his neighbour. I know
by mine own experience, that all flesh is in bondage under
sin, and cannot but sin, therefore am I merciful, and desire
God to loose the bonds of sin even in mine enemy.

GATHER not treasure together in earth, &c. (Mat. vi.)
but gather you treasure in heaven, &c. Let not your
hearts be glued to worldly things, study not to heap treasure
upon treasure, and riches upon riches, but study to bestow
well that which is gotten already, and let your abundance
succour the lack and need of the poor which have not.
Have an eye to good works, to which if ye have lust
and also power to do them, then are ye sure that the Spirit
of God is in you, and ye in Christ elect to the reward of
eternal life which followeth good works. But look that
thine eye be single and rob not Christ of his honour,
ascribe not that to the deserving of thy works, which is
given thee freely by the merits of his blood. In Christ we
are sons; in Christ we are heirs; in Christ God chose us
and elected us before the beginning of the world, created
us anew by the word of the gospel, and put his Spirit in

Margin notes:
But he of his mercy pardoneth us.

Mat. vi.

A true bestowing of alms.

In Christ we are all in all.

37

us for because we should do good works. A Christian man worketh, because it is the will of his Father only. If we do no good work, nor be merciful, how is our lust therein? If we have no lust to do good works, how is God's Spirit in us? If the Spirit of God be not in us, how are we his sons? How are we his heirs, and heirs annexed with Christ of the eternal life, which is promised to all them that believe in him? Now do our works testify and witness what we are, and what treasure is laid up for us in heaven, so that our eye be single, and look upon the commandment without respect of any thing save because it is God's will, and that God desireth it of us, and Christ hath deserved that we do it.

We must do good works because it is God's will that we should do them.

Not all they that say unto me, Lord, Lord, shall enter into the kingdom of heaven, but he that doth the will of my Father which is in heaven. (Mat. vii.) Though thou canst laud God with thy lips, and call Christ Lord, and canst babble and talk of the Scripture, and knowest all the stories of the Bible, yet shalt thou thereby never know thine election, or whether thy faith be right. But if thou feel lust in thine heart to the will of God, and bringest forth the fruits thereof, then hast thou confidence and hope; and thy deeds, and also the Spirit whence thy deeds spring certify thine heart that thou shalt enter, yea, art already entered into the kingdom of heaven. For it followeth, He that heareth the word and doth it buildeth his house upon a rock, and no tempest of temptations can overthrow it. For the Spirit of God is in his heart and comforteth him, and holdeth him fast to the rock of the merits of Christ's blood, in whom he is elect. Nothing is able to pluck him out of the hands of God, God is stronger than all things. And contrariwise, he that heareth the word, and doth it not, buildeth on the sand of his own imagination, and every tempest overthroweth his building. The cause is, he hath not God's Spirit in him, and therefore understandeth it not aright, neither worketh aright. For no man knoweth the things of God (saith

We must hear the word of God and do it.

38

Paul in the 1st Epistle to the Corinthians in the iind chap- 1 Cor. ii.
ter) save the Spirit of God, as no man knoweth what is in
a man but a man's spirit which is in him. So then if the
Spirit be not in a man he worketh not the will of God,
neither understandeth it, though he babble never so much
of the Scriptures. Nevertheless such a man may work after
his own imagination, but God's will can he not work, he
may offer sacrifice, but to do mercy knoweth he not. It is
easy to say unto Christ, Lord, Lord, but thereby shalt thou
never feel or be sure of the kingdom of heaven. But and if
thou do the will of God, then art thou sure that Christ is
thy Lord indeed and that thou in him art also a lord, in
that thou feelest thyself loosed and freed from the bondage
of sin, and lusty and of power to do the will of God.

Where the Spirit is there is feeling; for the Spirit maketh
us feel all things. Where the Spirit is not there is no feeling,
but a vain opinion or imagination. A physician serveth
but for sick men, and that for such sick men as feel their
sicknesses, and mourn therefore and long for health.
Christ likewise serveth but for sinners only as feel their sin,
and that for such sinners that sorrow and mourn in their
hearts for health. Health is power or strength to fulfil the
law, or to keep the commandments. Now he that longeth
for that health, that is to say, for to do the law of God, is
blessed in Christ, and hath a promise that his lust shall be
fulfilled, and that he shall be made whole. (Matt. v.)
Blessed are they which hunger and thirst for righteousness'
sake, (that is, to fulfil the law,) for their lust shall be fulfilled.
This longing and consent of the heart unto the law of God,
is the working of the Spirit which God hath poured into
thine heart, in earnest that thou mightest be sure that God
will fulfil all his promises that he hath made thee. It is
also the seal and mark which God putteth on all men
that he choseth unto everlasting life. So long as thou
seest thy sin and mournest and consentest to the law, and
longest (though thou be never so weak) yet the Spirit shall
keep thee in all temptations from desperation, and certify

Christ is
our only
Physician
to heal and
deliver us
of our sins.

thine heart that God for his truth shall deliver thee and save thee, yea, and by thy good deeds shalt thou be saved, not which thou hast done, but which Christ has done for thee, For Christ is thine and all his deeds are thy deeds. Christ is in thee and thou in him, knit together inseparably. Neither canst thou be damned except Christ be damned with thee: neither can Christ be saved except thou be saved with him.

Christ is
our anchor-
hold to sal-
vation.

Moreover thy heart is good, right, holy and just, for thy heart is no enemy to the law but a friend and a lover. The law and thy heart are agreed and at one, and therefore is God at one with thee. The consent of the heart unto the law, is unity and peace between God and man. For he is not mine enemy which would fain do me pleasure, and mourneth because he hath not wherewith. Now he that opened thy disease unto thee and made thee long for health, shall, as he hath promised, heal thee, and he that hath loosed thy heart, shall at his godly leisure, loose thy members. He that hath not the Spirit hath no feeling, neither lusteth or longeth after power to fulfil the law, neither abhorreth the pleasures of sin, neither hath any more certainty of the promises of God, than I have of a tale of Robin Hood, or of some jest that a man telleth me was done at Rome. Another man may lightly make me doubt or believe the contrary, seeing I have no experience thereof myself; so is it of them that feel not the working of the Spirit, and therefore in time of temptation the buildings of their imaginations fall.

A prophet,
what he is.

He that receiveth a prophet in the name of a prophet, that is, because he is a prophet, shall receive the reward of a prophet; and He that giveth one of these little ones a cup of cold water to drink in the name of a disciple, shall not loose his reward. (Matt. x.) Note this, that a prophet signifieth as well him that interpreteth the hard places of Scripture as him that prophesieth things to come. Now he that receiveth a prophet, a just man, or a disciple, shall have the same or like reward, that is to say, shall have the same eternal life which is appointed for them in Christ's blood

and merits. For except thou were elect to the same eternal
life and hadst the same faith and trust in God, and the same
Spirit, thou couldst never consent to their deeds and help
them. But thy deeds testify what thou art, and certify thy
conscience that thou art received to mercy, and sanctified
in Christ's passions and sufferings, and shalt hereafter, with
all them that follow God, receive the reward of eternal life.

Of thy words thou shalt be justified, and of thy words
thou shalt be condemned; (Matt. xii.) That is, thy words
as well as other deeds shall testify with thee or against thee
at the day of judgment. Many there are which abstain
from the outward deeds of fornication and adultery, nevertheless rejoice to talk thereof and laugh; their words and
laughter testify against them that their heart is impure, and
they adulterers and fornicators in the sight of God. The
tongue and other signs ofttimes utter the malice of the
heart though a man for many causes abstain his hand from
the outward deed or act.

Matt. xii.

The ab-staining from sin outwardly is but hy-pocrisy.

If thou wilt enter into life, keep the commandments;
(Matt. xix.) First, remember that when God commandeth
us to do any thing, he doth it not therefore because that we
of ourselves are able to do that he commandeth; but that
by the law we might see and know our horrible damnation
and captivity under sin, and [therefore] should repent and
come to Christ, and receive mercy and the Spirit of God to
loose us, strengthen us, and to make us able to do God's
will, which is the law. Now when he saith, If thou wilt enter into life keep the commandments, is as much [as] to say,
as he that keepeth the commandments is entered into life:
for except a man have first the Spirit of life in him by
Christ's purchasing, it is impossible for him to keep the
commandments, or that his heart should be loose or at liberty
to lust after them, for of nature we are enemies to the law
of God.

Matt. xix.

To believe unfeignedly in Christ is to keep the command-ments.

As touching that, Christ saith afterward, If thou wilt be
perfect go, and sell thy substance and give it to the poor;
he saith it not as who should say that there were any greater

41

perfection than to keep the law of God, (for that is all perfection,) but to shew the other his blindness, which saw not
that the law is spiritual, and requireth the heart. But
because he was not knowing that he had hurt any man with
the outward deed, he supposed that he loved his neighbour
as himself. But when he was bid to shew the deeds of
love, and give of his abundance to them that needed, he departed mourning. Which is an evident token that he
loved not his neighbour as well as himself. For if he had
need himself, it would not have grieved him to have received succour of another man. Moreover, he saw not that it
was murder and theft, that a man should have abundance
of riches lying by him, and not to shew mercy therewith,
and kindly to succour his neighbour's need. God hath
given one man riches to help another at need. If thy
neighbour need, and thou help him not, being able, thou
withholdest his duty from him, and art a thief before God.

That also, that Christ saith, how that it is harder for a
rich man (who loveth his riches so that he cannot find in
his heart liberally and freely to help the poor and needy)
to enter into the kingdom of heaven, than a camel to go
through the eye of a needle, declareth that he was not entered into the kingdom of heaven, that is to say, eternal
life. But he that keepeth the commandments is entered
into life, yea, hath life and the Spirit of life in him.

THIS kind of devils goeth not out but by prayer and
fasting. (Mat. xxvii.) Not that the devil is cast out by
merits of fasting or praying. For he saith before, that for
their unbelief's sake, they could not cast him out. It is
faith no doubt that casteth out the devils, and faith it is
that fasteth and prayeth. Faith hath the promises of God
whereunto she cleaveth, and in all things thirsteth [for] the
honour of God. She fasteth to subdue the body unto the
spirit that the prayer be not let, and that the spirit may
quietly talk with God: she also, whensoever opportunity is
given, prayeth God to fulfil his promises unto his praise

The law is spiritual and requireth the heart.

If the rich help not the poor in their need, they are but theives before God.

Mat. xxvii.

Faith casteth out devils.

Faith fasteth.

Faith prayeth.

and glory. And God, which is merciful in promising, and
true to fulfil them, casteth out the devils, and doth all that
faith desireth, and satisfieth her thirst.

COME, ye blessed of my Father, inherit the kingdom
prepared for you from the beginning of the world; for I
was athirst, and ye gave me drink, &c. (Mat. xxv.) Not *Mat. xxv.*
that a man with works deserveth eternal life as a workman
or labourer his hire or wages. Thou readest in the text,
that the kingdom was prepared for us from the beginning of
the world. And we are blessed and sanctified. In Christ's *In Christ's blood we are blessed from the curse of the law.*
blood are we blessed from that bitter curse and damnable
captivity under sin, wherein we were born and conceived.
And Christ's Spirit is poured into us, to bring forth good
works, and our works are the fruits of the Spirit, and the
kingdom is the deserving of Christ's blood, and so is faith
and the Spirit and good works also. Notwithstanding the
kingdom followeth good works, and good works testify that
we are heirs thereof, and at the day of judgment shall they
testify for the elect unto their comfort and glory: and to
the confusion of the ungodly, unbelieving and faithless
sinners, which had not trust in the word of God's promises, nor lust to the will of God; but were carried of
the spirit of their father the devil unto all abomination, to
work wickedness with all lust, delectation, and greediness.

MANY sins are forgiven her, for she loveth much;
(Luke vii.) Not that love was cause of forgiveness of sins, *Luke vii..*
but contrariwise the forgiveness of sins caused love, as it
followeth, to whom less was forgiven that same loveth less.
And afore he commended the judgment of Simon, which
answered that he loveth most to whom most was forgiven:
and also said at the last, Thy faith hath saved thee (or
made thee safe) go in peace. We cannot love except we
see some benefit and kindness. As long as we look on *The law condemneth.*
the law of God only, where we see but sin and damnation
and the wrath of God upon us, yea where we were damned

43

afore we were born we cannot love God. No, we cannot

The gospel comforteth and maketh us safe.

but hate him as a tyrant, unrighteous, unjust, and flee from him as did Cain. But when the gospel, that [those] glad tidings and joyful promises are preached, how that in Christ, God loveth us first, forgiveth us, and hath mercy on us, then love we again, and the deeds of our love declare our faith. This is the manner of speaking : as we say, Summer is nigh, for the trees blossom. Now is the blossoming of the trees not the cause that summer draweth nigh; but the drawing nigh of summer is the cause of the blossoms, and the blossoms put us in remembrance that summer is at hand. So Christ here teacheth Simon

Certain phrases of speech expounded.

by the ferventness of love in the outward deeds, to see a strong faith within whence so great love springeth. As the manner is to say, Do your charity, shew your charity, do a deed of charity, shew your mercy, do a deed of mercy, meaning thereby that our deeds declare how we love our neighbours, and how much we have compassion on them at their need. Moreover it is not possible to love except we see a cause. Except we see in our hearts the love and kindness of God to usward in Christ our Lord, it is not possible to love God aright.

We say also, He that loveth not my dog loveth not me. Not that a man should love my dog first, but if a man loved me, the love wherewith he loved me would compel him to love my dog, though the dog deserved it not, yea, though the dog had done him a displeasure, yet if he loved me, the same love would refrain him from revenging himself, and cause him to refer the vengeance unto me. Such

John iv.

speakings find we in Scripture ; John in the ivth of his first Epistle saith, He that saith I love God, and yet hateth his brother, is a liar ; For how can he that loveth not his brother whom he seeth, love God whom he seeth not? This is not spoken that a man should first love his brother and then God, but as it followeth : For this commandment have we of him, that he which loveth God should love his brother also. To love my neighbour is the commandment;

which commandment he that loveth not, loveth not God. The keeping of the commandment declareth what love I have to God. If I loved God purely, nothing that my neighbour could do were able to make me either to hate him, either to take vengeance on him myself, seeing that God hath commanded me to love him, and to remit all vengeance unto him. Mark now, how much I love the commandment, so much I love God; how much I love God, so much believe I that he is merciful, kind and good, yea, and a father unto me for Christ's sake. How much I believe that God is merciful unto me, and that he will for Christ's sake fulfil all his promises unto me ; so much I see my sins, so much do my sins grieve me, so much do I repent and sorrow that I sin, so much displeaseth me that poison that moveth me to sin, and so greatly desire I to be healed. So now by the natural order, first I see my sin ; then I repent and sorrow; then believe I God's promises, that he is merciful unto me, and forgiveth me, and will heal me at the last: then love I, and then I prepare myself to the commandment.

Where perfect love to God is, there are all good works.

THIS do and thou shalt live. (Luke x.) That is to say, Love thy Lord God with all thy heart, with all thy soul, and with all thy strength, and with all thy mind, and thy neighbour as thyself. As who should say, if thou do this, or though thou canst not do it, yet if thou feelest lust thereunto, and thy spirit sigheth, mourneth, and longeth after strength to do it, take a sign and evident token thereby, that the Spirit of life is in thee, and that thou art elect to life everlasting by Christ's blood, whose gift and purchase is thy faith, and that Spirit that worketh the will of God in thee, whose gift also are thy deeds, or rather the deeds of the Spirit of Christ, and not thine, and whose gift is the reward of eternal life, which followeth good works.

Luke x. What it is to love God with all our heart &c.

It followeth also in the same place of Luke, When he should depart he plucked out twopence and gave them to the host and said unto him, Take the charge or cure of him,

The true understanding of a parable.

and whatsoever thou spendest more I will recompense it thee at my coming again. Remember, this is a parable, and a parable may not be expounded word for word; but the intent of the similitude must be sought but only in the whole parable. The intent of the similitude is to shew to whom a man is a neighbour or who is a man's neighbour, which is both one, and what is to love a man's neighbour as himself.

The Samaritan helped him and shewed mercy as long as he was present, and when he could be no longer present, he left his money behind him, And if that were not sufficient, he left his credence to make good the rest, and forsook him not as long as the other had need. Then said Christ, Go thou and do likewise; that is, without difference or respection of persons : whosoever needeth thy help, him count thy neighbour, and his neighbour be thou, and shew mercy on him as long as he needeth thy succour, and that

We must ever be ready to help our neighbour.

is to love a man's neighbour as himself. Neighbour is a word of love, and signifieth that a man should be ever nigh and at hand, and ready to help in time of need.

They that will interpret parables word by word, fall into straights ofttimes, whence they cannot rid themselves; and preach lies instead of the truth. As do they which interpret by the twopence, the Old Testament and the New, and by that which is bestowed *Opera supererogationis.* Howbeit *Superarrogantia* were a meeter term. That is to say, deeds which are more than the law requireth, deeds of perfection and of liberality which a man is not bound to do but of his free will: and for them he shall have an higher place in heaven and may give to other of his merits; or of which the Pope after his death may give pardons from the pains of purgatory.

Against which exposition I answer; first, a greater perfection than the law is there not. A greater perfection than to love God and his will, which is the commandments, with all thine heart, with all thy soul, with all thy strength, with all thy mind, is there none; and to love a man's neighbour as himself is like the same. It is a wonderfu

46

love wherewith a man loveth himself. As glad as I would
be to receive pardon of mine own life, (if I had deserved
death) so glad ought I to be to defend my neighbour's life
without respect of my life, or of my good. A man ought
neither to spare his goods nor yet himself for his brother's
sake, after the ensample of Christ (1 John iii.) Herein *John iii.*
saith he, perceive we love, in that he, that is to say Christ,
gave his life for us, we ought therefore to bestow our lives
for the brethren. Now saith Christ, (John xv.) There is *John xv.*
no greater love than that a man bestow his life for his friend.

Moreover no man can fulfil the law, for John saith (1st *1st John i.*
chapter of the said Epistle,) If we say we have no sin, we
deceive ourselves and truth is not in us, if we knowledge
our sins, he is faithful and righteous to forgive us our sins
and to purge us from all iniquity. And in the Paternoster
also we say, Father, forgive us our sins. Now if we be all
sinners, none fulfilleth the law: for he that fulfilleth the law *Works that*
is no sinner. In the law: may neither Peter nor Paul nor *the Papists
called*
any other creature save Christ only rejoice. In the blood *works,
more than*
of Christ, which fulfilled the law for us, may every person *the law re-*
that repenteth, believeth, loveth the law, and mourneth for *quireth.*
strength to fulfil it, rejoice, be he never so weak a sinner.
The twopence therefore and the credence that he left behind him to bestow more, if need were, signifieth that he
was everywhere merciful, both present and absent, without
feigning, cloaking, complaining, or excusing, and forsake not
his neighbour as long as he has need. Which example I
pray God men may follow; and let *opera supererogationis*
alone.

MARY hath chosen a good part which shall not be taken
from her, (Luke x.) She was first chosen of God and called *Luke x.*
by grace, both to know her sin and also to hear the word
of faith, health, and glad tidings of mercy in Christ; and
faith was given her to believe, and the Spirit of God loosed
her heart from the bondage of sin: then consented she to
the will of God again, and above all things had delectation

to hear the word wherein she had obtained everlasting health, and namely, of his own mouth, which had purchased so great mercy for her.   God chooseth us first and loveth us first, and openeth our eyes to see his exceeding abundant love to us in Christ, and then love we again, and accept his will above all things, and serve him in that office whereunto he hath chosen us.

Sell that ye have, and give alms, and make you bags which wax not old, and treasure which faileth not in heaven. **Luke xii.** (Luke xii.) This and such like are not spoken that we should work as hirelings in respect of reward, and as though we should obtain heaven with merit: for he saith a little afore, Fear not, little flock, for it is your Father's pleasure to give **Whatsoever we have we receive it of the mercy and goodness of God.** you a kingdom. The kingdom cometh then of the good will of Almighty God through Christ, and such things are spoken partly to put us in remembrance of our duty to be kind again. As is that saying, Let your light so shine before men that they, seeing your good works, may glorify your Father which is in heaven : as who should say, if God hath given you so great gifts see ye be not unthankful, but **The great diversity and manner of the speaking of the Scriptures.** bestow them unto his praise. Some things are spoken to move us to put our trust in God, as are these ; Behold the lilies of the field : Behold the birds of the air : If your children ask you bread will ye proffer them a stone ? and many such like. Some are spoken to put us in remembrance to be sober, to watch and pray, and to prepare ourselves against temptations, and that we should understand and know how that temptations and occasion of evil come then most, when they are least looked for; lest we should be careless and sure of ourselves, negligent and unprepared. Some things are spoken that we should fear the wonderful and incomprehensible judgments of God lest we should presume. Some to comfort us that we despair not. And for like causes are all the ensamples of the Old Testament. In conclusion, the Scripture speaketh many things as the world speaketh, but they may not be worldly understood, but ghostly and spiritually, yea, the Spirit of God only un-

derstandeth them, and where he is not there is not the understanding of the Scripture; but unfruitful disputing and
brawling about words.

The Scripture saith, God seeth, God heareth, God smel-
leth, God walketh, God is with them, God is not with
them, God is angry, God is pleased, God sendeth his Spirit,
God taketh his Spirit away, and a thousand such like: and
yet is none of them true after the worldly manner, and as the
words sound. Read the iind chapter of Paul to the Cor-
rinthians: The natural man understandeth not the things
of God, but the Spirit of God only. And we, saith he, have
received the Spirit which is of God to understand the things
which are given us of God: or without the Spirit it is impossible to understand them. Read also the viiith to the
Romans: They that are led with the Spirit of God, are
the sons of God: now the son knoweth his father's will
and the servant that hath not the Spirit of Christ, (saith
Paul) is none of his: likewise he that hath not the Spirit
of God, is none of God's, for it is both one Spirit, as thou
mayest see in the same place.

Now he that is of God heareth the word of God, (John
viii.) And who is of God but he that hath the Spirit of God?
furthermore, saith he, Ye hear it not, because ye are not
of God; that is, ye have no lust in the word of God, for ye
understand it not, and that because his Spirit is not in you.

Forasmuch then as the Scripture is nothing else but that
which the Spirit of God hath spoken by the prophets and
apostles, and cannot be understood but of the same Spirit,
Let every man pray to God to send him his Spirit to loose
him from his natural blindness and ignorance, and to give
him understanding, and feeling of the things of God, and of
the speaking of the Spirit of God. And mark this process:
first, we are damned of nature, so conceived and born, as
a serpent is a serpent, and a toad a toad, and a snake a
snake by nature. And as thou seest a young child which
hath pleasure in many things wherein is present death, as in
fire, water, and so forth, would slay himself with a thousand

Marginal notes:

The sayings of the Scriptures may not be grossly un-
derstoood.

The natural man under-
standeth not the things of God.

Rom. viii.

John viii.

The Scrip-
ture is no-
thing else
but that
which the
Spirit of
God hath
spoken.

49

deaths if he were not waited upon and kept therefrom, even so we, if we should live these thousand years, could in all that time delight in no other thing, nor yet seek any other thing but that wherein is death of the soul.

Secondarily, of the whole multitude of the nature of man, whom God hath elect and chosen, and to whom he hath appointed mercy and grace in Christ, to them sendeth he his Spirit, which openeth their eyes, sheweth them their misery, and bringeth them unto the knowledge of themselves, so that they hate and abhor themselves, are astonished and amazed, and at their wit's end, neither wot what to do, or where to seek health. Then lest they should flee from God by desperation, he comforteth them again with his sweet promises in Christ, and certifieth their hearts that for Christ's sake they are received to mercy, and their sins forgiven, and they elect and made the sons of God, and heirs with Christ of eternal life: and thus, through faith, are they set at peace with God.

By faith in Christ we are brought to the state of salvation.

Now may not we ask why God chooseth one and not another; either think that God is unjust to damn us afore we do any actual deed; seeing that God hath power over all his creatures of right to do with them what he list, or to make of every one of them as he listeth. Our darkness cannot perceive his light. God will be feared, and not have his secret judgments known. Moreover we by the light of faith see a thousand things which are impossible to an infidel to see: so likewise no doubt, in the light of the clear vision of God, we shall see things which now God will not have known. For pride ever accompanieth high knowledge, but grace accompanieth meekness. Let us therefore give diligence rather to do the will of God, than to search his secrets which are not profitable for us to know.

God worketh his own will with all his creatures.

When we are thus reconciled to God, made the friends of God and heirs of eternal life, the Spirit that God hath poured into us testifieth that we may not live after our old deeds of ignorance: for how is it possible that we should repent and abhor them, and yet have lust to live in them?

If we believe in God we must put off the old man and his works.

50

We are sure therefore that God hath created and made us new in Christ and put his Spirit in us that we should live a new life which is the life of good works.

That thou mayest know what are good works, and the intent of good works, or wherefore good works serve, mark this that followeth.

The life of a Christian man is inward between him and God, and properly is the consent of the Spirit to the will of God and to the honour of God. And God's honour is the final end of all good works. *Good works what they are, and to what end they serve.*

Good works are all things that are done within the laws of God, in which God is honoured, and for which thanks are given to God.

Fasting is to abstain from surfeiting, or overmuch eating, from drunkenness, and care of the world (as thou mayest read Luke xxi.) and the end of fasting is to tame the body that the Spirit may have a free course to God, and may quietly talk with God. For overmuch eating and drinking, and care of worldly business, press down the spirit, choke her and tangle her that she cannot lift up herself to God. Now he that fasteth for any other intent than to subdue the body that the Spirit may wait on God, and freely excercise herself in the things of God; the same is blind, and wotteth not what he doth, erreth and shooteth at a wrong mark, and his intent and imagination is abominable in the sight of God. When thou fastest from meat and drinkest all day, is that a Christian fast? either to eat at one meal that were sufficient for four? A man at four times may bear that he cannot at once. Some fast from meat and drink, and yet so tangle themselves in worldly business that they cannot once think on God. Some abstain from butter, some from eggs, some from all manner [of] white meat, some this day, some that day, some in the honour of this saint, some of that, and every man for a sundry purpose. Some for the tooth ache, some for the head ache, for fevers, pestilence, for sudden death, for hanging, drowning, and to be delivered from the pains of *Fasting, the true use thereof.*

True fasting what it is.

Superstitious fasting.

hell. Some are so mad, that they fast one of the Thursdays between the two St. Mary days, in the worship of that saint, whose day is hallowed between Christmas and Candlemas; and that to be delivered from the pestilence. All those men fast without conscience of God, and without knowledge of the true intent of fasting, and do no other than honour saints, as the Gentiles and heathen worshipped their idols, and are drowned in blindness, and know not of the Testament, that God hath made to man ward in Christ's blood. In God have they neither hope nor confidence, neither believe his promises, neither know his will, but are yet in captivity under the prince of darkness.

Superstitious watching.

WATCH, is not only to abstain from sleep, but also to be circumspect and to cast all perils; as a man should watch a tower or a castle. We must remember that the snares of the devil are infinite and innumerable, and that every moment arise new temptations, and that in all places meet us fresh occasions; against which we must prepare

True watching.

ourselves and turn to God and complain to him, and make our moan, and desire him of his mercy to be our shield, our tower, our castle, and defence from all evil, to put his strength in us, for without him we can do nought, and above all things we must call to mind what promises God hath made and what he hath sworn that he will do to us for Christ's sake, and with strong faith cleave unto him and desire him of his mercy and for the love that he hath to Christ, and for his truth's sake, to fulfil his promises. If we thus cleave to God with strong faith and believe his words, then as saith Paul, (1st Cor. x.) God is faithful that he will not suffer us to be tempted above that we are able, or above our might, that is to say, if we cleave to his promises and not to our own fantasies and imaginations, he will put might and power into us that shall be stronger than all the temptation which he shall suffer to be against us.

Prayer, what it is.

PRAYER is a mourning, a longing, and a desire of the

man mourneth and sorroweth in his heart, longing for
health.   Faith ever prayeth.   For after that by faith we
are reconciled to God, and have received mercy and forgiveness of God, the spirit longeth and thirsteth for
strength to do the will of God, and that God may be
honoured, his name hallowed, and his pleasure and will
fulfilled.   The spirit waiteth and watcheth on the will of
God, and ever hath her own fragility and weakness before
her eyes ; and when she seeth temptation and peril draw
nigh, she turneth to God, and to the Testament that God
hath made to all that believe and trust in Christ's blood,
and desireth God for his mercy, and truth, and for the love he
hath to Christ, that he will fulfil his promise, that he will
succour, and help, and give us strength, and that he will sanc-
tify his name in us, and fulfil his godly will in us, and that
he will not look on our sin and iniquity, but on his mercy,
on his truth, and on the love that he oweth to his Son
Christ, and for his sake to keep us from temptation, that
we be not overcome, and that he deliver us from evil, and
whatsoever moveth us contrary to his godly will.

Moreover, of his own experience he feeleth other men's   True prayer
need, and no less commendeth to God the infirmities of
other than his own, knowing that there is no strength, no
help, no succour, but of God only.   And as merciful as
he feeleth God in his heart to himselfward, so merciful is
he to other ; and as greatly as he feeleth his own misery,
so great compassion hath he on other.   His neighbour is
no less care to him than himself : he feeleth his neighbour's
grief no less than his own.   And whensoever he seeth occasion, he cannot but pray for his neighbour as well as
for himself : his nature is to seek the honour of God in
all men, and to draw (as much as in him is) all men unto
God.   This is the law of love, which springeth out of
Christ's blood into the hearts of all them that have their
trust in him.   No man needeth to bid a Christian man to pray,
if he see his neighbour's need : if he see it not, put him in
remembrance only, and then he cannot but do his duty.

Now, as touching we desire one another to pray for us, that do we to put our neighbour in remembrance of his duty, and not that we trust in his holiness. Our trust is in God, in Christ, and in the truth of God's promises; we have also a promise, that when two or three, or more, agree together in any thing, according to the will of God, God heareth us. Notwithstanding, as God heareth many, so heareth he few, and so heareth he one, if he pray after the will of God, and desire the honour of God. He that desireth mercy, the same feeleth his own misery and sin, and mourneth in his heart for to be delivered, that he might honour God; and God for his truth must hear him, which saith by the mouth of Christ, (Matt. v.) Blessed are they that hunger and thirst after righteousness, for they shall be filled. God, for his truth's sake, must put the righteousness of Christ in him, and wash his unrighteousness away in the blood of Christ. And be the sinner never so weak, never so feeble and frail, sin he never so oft and so grievous, yet so long as this lust, desire, and mourning to be delivered remaineth in him, God seeth not his sins, reckoneth them not, for his truth's sake, and love to Christ. He is not a sinner in the sight of God that would be no sinner. He that would be delivered hath his heart loose already. His heart sinneth not, but mourneth, repenteth, and consenteth unto the law and will of God, and justifieth God; that is, beareth record that God which made the law is righteous and just. And such an heart, trusting in Christ's blood, is accepted for full righteous. And his weakness, infirmity, and frailty is pardoned, and his sins not looked upon: until God put more strength in him, and fulfil his lust.

When the weak in the faith, and unexpert in the mysteries of Christ, desire us to pray for them, then ought we to lead them to the truth and promises of God, and teach them to put their trust in the promises of God, in love that God hath to Christ and to us for his sake, and to strengthen their weak consciences, shewing and proving by

the Scripture, that as long as they follow the Spirit and
resist sin, it is impossible they should fall so deep that
God shall not pull them up again, if they hold fast by the
anchor of faith, having trust and confidence in Christ.
The love that God hath to Christ is infinite; and Christ
did and suffered all things not for himself, to obtain favour
or aught else; for he had ever the full favour of God, and
was ever Lord over all things; but to reconcile us to God,
and to make us heirs with him of his Father's kingdom.
And God hath promised, that whosoever calleth on his
name shall never be confounded or ashamed. (Rom. ix.)   Rom. ix.
If the righteous fall (saith the Scripture) he shall not be
bruised; the Lord shall put his hand under him. Who is
righteous but he that trusteth in Christ's blood, be he
never so weak?   Christ is our righteousness; and in him   Christ is
ought we to teach all men to trust, and to expound unto   our righte-
                                                            ousness.
all men the Testament, that God hath made to us sinners
in Christ's blood. This ought we to do, and not make a
prey of them to lead them captive, to sit in their consciences,
and to teach them to trust in our holiness, good deeds and
prayers, to the intent that we would feed our idle and slow
bellies of their great labour and sweat, and so to make
ourselves Christs and Saviours. For if I take on me to
save other by my merits, make I not myself a Christ
and a Saviour, and am indeed a false prophet, and a true
Antichrist, and exalt myself and sit in the temple of God;
that is to wit, the consciences of men?

Among Christian men, love maketh all things common;   Love
every man is other's debtor, and every man is bound   among
to minister to his neighbour, and to supply his neigh-   Christian
bour's lack of that wherewith God hath endowed   men mak-
                                                    eth all
him. As thou seest in the world, how the lords and   things
officers minister peace in the commonwealth, punish   common.
murderers, thieves, and evil doers, and to maintain their
order and estate, do the commons minister to them again
rent, tribute, toll, and custom: so in the gospel, the curates
which in every parish preach the gospel, ought of duty to

receive an honest living for them and their households ; and even so ought the other officers, which are necessarily required in the commonwealth of Christ. We need not to use filthy lucre in the gospel, to chop and change, and to play the taverners, altering the word of God as they do their wines, to their most advantage, and to fashion God's word after every man's mouth ; or to abuse the name of Christ, to obtain thereby authority and power to feed our slow bellies. Now seest thou what prayer is, the end thereof, and wherefore it serveth.

Man's imagination cannot alter the law of God, neither make it more or less.

If thou give me a thousand pounds to pray for thee, I am no more bound than I was before. Man's imagination can make the commandment of God neither greater nor smaller, neither can to the law of God either add or minish. God's commandment is as great as himself. I am bound to love the Turk with all my might and power ; yea, and above my power, even from the ground of my heart, after the ensample that Christ loved me,—neither to spare goods, body, or life, to win him to Christ. And what can I do more for thee if thou gavest me all the world ? Where I see need there can I not but pray, if God's Spirit be in me.

Alms, what it is.

Alms is a Greek word, and signifieth mercy. One Christian is debtor to another at his need, of all that he is able to do for him, until his need be sufficed. Every Christian man ought to have Christ always before his eyes, as an ensample to counterfeit and follow, and to do to his neighbour as Christ hath done to him, as Paul teacheth in all his epistles, and Peter in his first, and John in his first also. This order useth Paul in all his epistles : first, he preacheth the law, and proveth that the whole nature of man is damned, in that the heart lusteth contrary to the will of God. For if we were of God, no doubt we should have lust in his will. Then preacheth he Christ, the gospel, the promises, and the mercy that God hath set forth to all men in Christ's blood : which they that believe, and take it for an earnest thing, turn themselves to God, begin to love God again, and to prepare themselves to his

1 Pet. i.
1 John i.

56

will by the working of the Spirit of God in them. Last of all, exhorteth he to unity, peace, and soberness; to avoid brawlings, sects, opinions, disputing and arguing about words, and to walk in the plain and single faith and feeling of the Spirit, and to love one another after the ensample of Christ, even as Christ loved us; and to be thankful, and to walk worthy of the gospel, and as it becometh Christ, and with the ensample of pure living to draw all to Christ.

Christ is Lord over all; and every Christian is heir annexed with Christ, and therefore Lord of all; and every one Lord of whatsoever another hath. If thy brother or neighbour therefore need, and thou have to help him, and yet shewest not mercy, but withdrawest thy hands from him, then robbest thou him of his own, and art a thief. A Christian man hath Christ's spirit. Now is Christ a merciful thing: if, therefore, thou be not merciful, after the ensample of Christ, then hast thou not his Spirit. If thou have not Christ's Spirit, then art thou none of his, (Rom. viii.) nor hast any part with him. Moreover, though thou shew mercy unto thy neighbour, yet if thou do it not with such burning love as Christ did unto thee, so must thou knowledge thy sin, and desire mercy in Christ. A Christian man hath nought to rejoice in, as concerning his deeds. His rejoicing is that Christ died for him, and that he is washed in Christ's blood. Of his deeds rejoiceth he not, neither counteth his merits, neither giveth pardons of them, neither seeketh an higher place in heaven of them, neither maketh himself a saviour of other men through his good works: but giveth all honour to God, and in his greatest deeds of mercy, knowledgeth himself a sinner unfeignedly, and is abundantly content with that place that is prepared for him of Christ; and his good deeds are to him a sign only that Christ's Spirit is in him, and he in Christ, and, through Christ, elect to eternal life.

The order of love or charity which some dream, the gospel of Christ knoweth not of, that a man should begin at himself, and serve himself first, and then descend, I wot

He that is merciful hath the Spirit of God.

Rom. viii.

Love seeketh not her own profit.

not by what steps. Love seeketh not her own profit, (1 Cor.

1 Cor.xiii. xiii.) but maketh a man to forget himself, and to turn his profit to another man, as Christ sought not himself, or his own profit, but ours. This term, myself, is not in the gospel; neither yet father, mother, sister, brother, kinsman, that one should be preferred in love above another.

Christ is all in all things. But Christ is all in all things. Every Christian man to another is Christ himself; and thy neighbour's need hath as good right in thy goods as hath Christ himself, which is heir and Lord over all. And look, what thou owest to Christ, that thou owest to thy neighbour's need: to thy neighbour owest thou thine heart, thyself, and all that thou hast and canst do. The love that springeth out of Christ excludeth no man, neither putteth difference between one and another. In Christ we are all of one degree, without respect of persons. Notwithstanding, though a Christian man's heart be open to all men, and receiveth all men, yet, because that his ability of goods extendeth not so far, this *Every one must care for their own households.* provision is made,—that every man shall care for his own household, as father and mother, and thine elders that have holpen thee, wife, children, and servants. If thou shouldest not care and provide for thine household, then were thou an infidel, seeing thou hast taken on thee so to do, and forasmuch as that is thy part committed to thee of the *First look to thine own house-hold, and then to the poor.* congregation. When thou hast done thy duty to thine household, and yet hast further abundance of the blessing of God, that owest thou to the poor that cannot labour, or would labour and can get no work, and are destitute of friends; to the poor, I mean, which thou knowest, to them of thine own parish. For that provision ought to be had in the congregation, that every parish care for their poor. If thy neighbours which thou knowest be served, and thou yet have superfluity, and hearest necessity to be among the brethren a thousand miles of, to them art thou debtor. Yea, to the very infidels we be debtors, if they need, as far forth as we maintain them not against Christ, or to blaspheme Christ. Thus is every man that needeth thy

help, thy father, mother, sister and brother in Christ ; even
as every man that doth the will of the father, is father,
mother, sister and brother unto Christ. .

Moreover if any be an infidel and a false christian, and
forsake his household, his wife, children, and such as cannot help themselves, then art thou bound and thou have
wherewith even as much as to thine own household. And
they have as good right in thy goods as thou thyself:
and if thou withdraw mercy from them, and hast wherewith
to help them, then art thou a thief. If thou shew mercy,
so doest thou thy duty, and art a faithful minister in the
household of Christ, and of Christ shalt thou have thy reward and thanks. If the whole world were thine, yet hath
every brother his right in thy goods, and is heir with thee,
as we are all heirs with Christ. Moreover the rich and they
that have wisdom with them must see the poor set a work,
that as many as are able may feed themselves with the labour of their own hands, according to the Scripture and
commandment of God.

We must for Christ's sake shew our compassion and charity to all men, so far as our ability will extend.

Now seest thou what alms-deeds meaneth, and wherefore
it serveth. He that seeketh with his alms more than to be merciful to a neighbour, to succour his brother's need, to do his
duty to his brother, to give his brother that he oweth him,
the same is blind and seeth not what it is to be a christian
man, and to have fellowship in Christ's blood.

As pertaining to good works, understand that all works
are good which are done within the law of God, in faith
and with thanksgiving to God, and understand that thou in
doing them pleasest God, whatsoever thou doest within the
law of God, as when thou makest water. And trust me, if
either wind or water were stopped, thou shouldest feel what
a precious thing it were to do either of both, and what
thanks ought to be given God therefore. Moreover put
no difference between works, but whatsoever cometh into
thy hands that do, as time, place, and occasion giveth, and
as God hath put thee in degree high or low. For as
touching to please God, there is no work better than

Good works what they are.

another. God looketh not first on thy work as the world doth, as though the beautifulness of the work pleased him as it doth the world, or as though he had need of them : but God looketh first on thy heart, what faith thou hast to his words, how thou believest him, trustest him, and how thou lovest him for his mercy that he hath showed thee ; he looketh with what heart thou workest, and not what thou workest, how thou acceptest the degree that he hath put thee in, and not of what degree thou art, whether thou be an apostle or a shoemaker. Set this ensample before thine eyes. Thou art a kitchen page, and washest thy master's dishes, another is an apostle, and preacheth the word of God. Of

2 Cor. ix. this apostle hark what Paul saith in the iind Cor. ix. If I preach, saith he , I have nought to rejoice in, for necessity is put unto me; as who should say, God hath made me so. Woe is unto me if I preach not. If I do it willingly, saith he, then have 1 my reward, that is, then am I sure that God's Spirit is in me and that I am elect to eternal life. If I do it against my will, an office is committed unto me; that is, if I do it not of love to God, but to get a living thereby, and for a worldly purpose, and had rather otherwise live, then do I that office which God hath put me in, and yet please not God myself. Note now, if this apostle preach not, as many do not, which not only make themselves apostles, but also compel men to take them for greater than apostles, yea, for greater than Christ himself : then woe is unto him, that is, his damnation is just. If he preach and his heart not right, yet ministereth he the office that God hath put him in, and they that have the Spirit of God, hear the voice of God, yea, though he speak in an ass. More-

We must do good works and yet put no trust in them. over howsoever he preacheth he hath not to rejoice in that he preacheth. But and if he preach willingly, with a true heart, and of concience to God, then hath he his reward, that is, then feeleth he the earnest of eternal life, and the working of the Spirit of God in him. And as he feeleth God's goodness and mercy, so be thou sure he feeleth his own infirmity, weakness, and unworthiness, and mourneth

and knowledgeth his sin, in that the heart will not arise to
work with that full lust and love that is in Christ our
Lord: And nevertheless is yet at peace with God, through
faith and trust in Christ Jesu.   For the earnest of the Spirit that worketh in him, testifieth and beareth witness unto
his heart that God hath chosen him, and that his grace shall
suffice him, which grace is now not idle in him.   In his
works putteth he his trust.

Now thou that ministerest in the kitchen, and art but a
kitchen page, receivest all things of the hand of God,
knowest that God hath put thee in that office, submittest thyself to his will and servest thy master not as a man, but as
Christ himself with a pure heart, according as Paul
teacheth us, puttest thy trust in God, and with him seekest
thy reward.   Moreover there is not a good deed done, but
thy heart rejoiceth therein, yea, when thou hearest that the
word of God is preached by this apostle and seest the
people turn to God, thou consentest unto the deed; thine
heart breaketh out in joy, springeth and leapeth in thy breast,
that God is honoured: and in thine heart doest the same
that that apostle doth, and haply with greater delectation,
and a more fervent spirit.   Now he that receiveth a prophet
in the name of a prophet shall receive the reward of a
prophet; (Matt. x.) that is, he hath consenteth to the deed
of a prophet, and maintaineth it, the same hath the same
Spirit and earnest of everlasting life, which the prophet
hath, and is elect as the prophet is.

God is no accepter of persons, but receiveth all that submit themselves unto him.

Matt. x.

Now if thou compare deed to deed, there is difference
betwixt washing of dishes, and preaching of the word of
God; but as touching to please God none at all: for
neither that nor this pleaseth, but as far forth as God hath
chosen a man, hath put his Spirit in him, and purified his
heart by faith and trust in Christ.

Let every man therefore wait on the office wherein Christ
hath put him, and therein serve his brethren.   If he be of
low degree let him patiently therein abide, till God pro-
mote him, and exalt him higher.   Let kings and head officers

As all deeds are acceptable to God that are done in faith, so no deed is allowed good in God's sight (how glorious to the world soever it appears) if it be without faith.

seek Christ in their offices, and minister peace and quiet-
ness unto the brethren; punish sin, and that with mercy,
even with the same sorrow and grief of mind as they would
cut off a finger or joint, a leg or arm, of their own body,
if there were such disease in them that either they must be
cut off, or else all the body must perish.

Every man
to walk
truly in his
vocation,
is the right
service of
God.

Let every man of whatsoever craft or occupation he be
of, whether brewer, baker, tailor, victualler, merchant, or
husbandman, refer his craft and occupation unto the commonwealth, and serve his brethren as he would do Christ
himself. Let him buy and sell truly, and not set dice on
his brethren; and so sheweth he mercy, and his occupation
pleaseth God. And when thou receivest money for thy labour or ware thou receivest thy duty. For wherein soever
thou minister to thy brethren, thy brethren are debtors to
give thee wherewith to maintain thyself and household.
And let your superfluities succour the poor, of which sort
shall ever be some in all towns, and cities, and villages, and
that I suppose the greatest number. Remember that we

We must
be merciful
one to
another.

are members of one body, and ought to minister one to
another mercifully: and remember that whatsoever we have
it is given us of God, to bestow it on our brethren. Let
him that eateth, eat and give God thanks, only let not thy
meat pull thine heart from God; and let him that drinketh
do likewise. Let him that hath a wife, give God thanks for
his liberty, only let not thy wife withdraw thine heart from
God, and then pleasest thou God, and hast the word of God
for thee. And in all things look on the word of God, and
therein put thy trust, and not in a visor, in a disguised gar-
ment, and a cut shoe.

Seek the word of God in all things, and without the
word of God do nothing, though it appear never so glorious.
Whatsoever is done without the word of God that count

Luke xvii.

idolatry. The kingdom of heaven is within us. (Luke xvii.)
Wonder therefore at no monstrous shape, nor at any outward thing without the word: for the world was never drawn
from God but with an outward shew and glorious appearance

and shining of hypocrisy, and of feigned and visored fasting, praying, watching, singing, offering, sacrificing, hallowing of superstitious ceremonies, and monstrous disguising.

Hypocrites are vainglorious in all their works.

Take this for an ensample: John Baptist which had testimony of Christ and of the gospel, that there never rose a greater among womens' children, with his fasting, watching, praying, rayment, and strait living, deceived the Jews, and brought them in doubt whether John were very Christ or not, and yet no Scripture or miracle testifying it, so greatly the blind nature of man looketh on the outward shining of works and regardeth not the inward word which speaketh to the heart. When they sent to John asking him whether he were Christ, he denied it. When they asked him what he was, and what he said of himself? he answered not, I am he that watcheth, prayeth, drinketh no wine nor strong drink, eateth neither fish nor flesh, but live with wild honey and grasshoppers, and wear a coat of camel's hair and a girdle of a skin; but said, I am a voice of a crier. My voice only pertaineth to you. Those outward things ye wonder at, pertain to myself, only unto the taming of my body. To you am I a voice only, and that which I preach. My preaching (if it be received into a penitent or repenting heart) shall teach you how to live and please God, according as God shall shed out his grace on every man. John preached repentance, saying, Prepare the Lord's way and make his paths straight. The Lord's way is repentance, and not hypocrisy of man's imagination, and invention. It is not possible that the Lord Christ should come to a man, except he know himself and his sin, and truly repent: make his paths straight:—the paths are the law, if you understand it aright as God hath given it. Christ saith in the xviith of Matt. Elias shall first come, that is, shall come before Christ, and restore all things, meaning of John Baptist. John Baptist did restore the law and the Scripture unto the right sense and understanding, which the Pharisees partly had darkened and made of none effect through their own traditions; (Matt. xv.) Where Christ rebuketh them saying

True preachers must preach repentance.

Matt. xvii.

Matt. xv.

Why transgress ye the commandments of God through your traditions? and partly had corrupted it with glosses and false interpretations, that no man could understand it.

Matt. xxiii.

Wherefore Christ rebuketh them, (Matt. xxiii.) saying, Woe be to you pharisees, hypocrites, which shut up the kingdom of heaven before men: ye enter not yourselves, neither suffer them that come to enter in: and partly did beguile the people

The manner and doctrine of hypocrites.

and blind their eyes in disguising themselves, as thou readest in the same xxiiird chapter, how they made broad and large phylacteries, and did all their works to be seen of men, that the people should wonder at their disguisings and visoring themselves otherwise than God hath made them: and partly mocked them with hypocrisy of false holiness, in fasting,

Matt. vi.

praying, and alms-giving; (Matt. vi.) And this did they for lucre, to be in authority, to sit in the consciences of people, and to be counted as God himself, that people should trust in their holiness, and not in God, as thou readest in the

Matt. xxiii.

place above rehearsed; (Matt. xxiii.) Woe be to you pharisees, hypocrites, which devour widows' houses under a colour of a long prayer. Counterfeit therefore nothing without the word of God, when thou understandest that it shall teach thee all things, how to apply outward things and whereunto to refer them. Beware of thy good intent, good mind, good affection, or zeal, as they call it. Peter of a good

Matt. xvi.

mind and of a good affection or zeal, chid Christ, (Matt. xvi.) because that he said he must go to Jerusalem, and there be slain; but Christ called him Satan for his labour, a name that belongeth to the devil, and said, That he perceived not godly things but worldly. Of a good intent, and of a fervent affection to Christ, the sons of Zebedee would have had fire to come down from heaven to consume the Samaritans,

Luke ix.

(Luke ix.) but Christ rebuked them, saying that they wist not of what Spirit they were: that is, that they understood not how that they were altogether worldly and fleshly minded. Peter smote Malchus of a good zeal, but Christ condemned his deed. The very Jews of a good intent and of a good zeal slew Christ and persecuted the apostles as

64

Paul beareth them record; (Rom. x.) I bear them record
(saith he) that they have a fervent mind to Godward, but
not according to knowledge. It is another thing then, to
do of a good mind, and to do of knowledge. Labour
for knowledge that thou mayest know God's will, and
what he would have thee to do. Our mind, intent and
affection or zeal, are blind, and all that we do of them is
damned of God, and for that cause hath God made a
testament between him and us, wherein is contained both
what he would have us to do, and what he would have us
to ask of him. See therefore that thou do nothing to
please God withal but that he commandeth, neither ask
any thing of him, but that he hath promised thee. The
Jews also as it appeareth (Acts vii.) slew Stephen of a
good zeal; because he proved, by the Scripture, that God
dwelleth not in churches or temples made with hands.
The churches at the beginning were ordained, that the
people should thither resort to hear the word of God there
preached only, and not for the use wherein they now are.
The temple wherein God will be worshipped, is the heart
of man. For God is a Spirit (saith Christ, John iv.) and
will be worshipped in the Spirit and in truth: that is,
when a penitent heart consenteth unto the law of God,
and with a strong faith longeth for the promises of God.
So is God honoured on all sides, in that we count him
righteous in all his laws and ordinances, and also trust in
all his promises. Other worshipping of God is there
none, except we make an idol of him.

IT shall be recompensed thee, at the rising again of
the righteous. (Luke xiv.) Read the text before, and
thou shalt perceive that Christ doth here that same that he
doth Mat. v. that is, he putteth us in remembrance of our
duty, that we be to the poor as Christ is to us, and also
teacheth us, how that we can never know whether our
love be right, and whether it spring of Christ or no, as long
as we are but kind to them only which do as much for us

No zeal without knowledge is good.
Churches, why they were first ordained.
The true temple of God is the heart of man.
Luke xvi.
Mat. v.

65

again. But and we be merciful to the poor, for conscience to God, and of compassion and hearty love, which compassion and love spring of the love we have to God in Christ, for the pure mercy and love that he hath shewed on us: then have we a sure token that we are beloved of God, and washed in Christ's blood, and elect by Christ's deserving unto eternal life.

The Scripture speaketh as a father doth to his young son, Do this or that, and then will I love thee; yet the father loveth his son first, and studieth with all his power and wit to overcome his child with love, and with kindness to make him do that which is comely, honest, and good for itself. A kind father and mother love their children even when they are evil, that they would shed their blood to make them better, and to bring them into the right way. And a natural child studieth not to obtain his father's love with works, but considereth with what love his father loveth him withal, and therefore loveth again, is glad to do his father's will, and studieth to be thankful.

The spirit of the world understandeth not the speaking of God, neither the spirit of the wise of this world, neither the spirit of philosophers, neither the spirit of Socrates, of Plato, or of Aristotle's Ethics, as thou mayest see in the first and second chapter of the first to the Corinthians. Though that many are not ashamed to rail and blaspheme, saying, How should he understand the Scripture seeing he is no philosopher, neither hath seen his metaphysic? Moreover they blaspheme, saying, How can he be a divine, and wotteth not what is *subjectum in theologia*? Nevertheless as a man, without the spirit of Aristotle or philosophy, may by the Spirit of God understand Scripture: even so by the Spirit of God understandeth he that God is to be sought in all the Scripture, and in all things, and yet wotteth not what meaneth *subjectum in theologia*, because it is a term of their own making. If thou shouldest say to him that hath the Spirit of God, the love of God is the keeping of the commandments, and to

The manner of the speaking of the Scripture.

The wise of this world do not understand the speaking of God in his Scriptures.

The Papists' arguments.

66

love a man's neighbour is to shew mercy, he would, without
arguing or disputing, understand, how that of the love of
God springeth the keeping of his commandments, and of
the love to thy neighbour springeth mercy.   Now would
Aristotle deny such speaking, and a Dun's man would
make twenty distinctions.   If thou shouldest say, (as saith
John in the ivth of his Epistle) How can he that loveth
not his neighbour whom he seeth, love God whom he seeth
not?   Aristotle would say, Lo, a man must first love his
neighbour and then God, and out of the love to thy neighbour springeth the love to God.   But he that feeleth the
working of the Spirit of God, and also from what vengeance the blood of Christ hath delivered him, understandeth
how that it is impossible to love either father or mother,
sister, brother, neighbour, or his own self aright, except it
spring out of the love to God, and perceiveth that the love
to a man's neighbour is a sign of the love to God, as good
fruit declareth a good tree, and that the love to a man's
neighbour accompanieth and followeth the love of God, as
heat accompanieth and followeth fire.

Likewise when the Scripture saith, Christ shall reward
every man at the resurrection, or uprising again, according
to his deeds, the spirit of Aristotle's Ethics would say,
Lo, with the multitude of good works mayest thou, and
must thou, obtain everlasting life.   And also a place in
heaven high or low, according as thou hast many or few
good works: and yet wotteth not what a good work
meaneth, as Christ speaketh of good works, as he that
seeth not the heart, but outward things only.   But he
that hath God's Spirit understandeth it.   He feeleth that
good works are nothing but fruits of love, compassion,
mercifulness, and of a tenderness of heart which a
Christian hath to his neighbour, and that love springeth
of that love which he hath to God, to his will and commandments, and understandeth also, that the love which
man hath to God springeth of the infinite love and bot-
tomless mercy which God in Christ shewed first to us,

Aristotle's and Papists' doctrine.

Good works are the fruits of love.

as saith John in the Epistle and Chapter above rehearsed. In this (saith he) appeareth the love of God to usward, because that God sent his only begotten Son into the world that we ·might live through him.   Herein is love,

God first loved us, and not we him.

not that we loved God, but that he loved us, and sent his Son to make agreement for our sins.   In conclusion, a Christian man feeleth that that unspeakable love and mercy which God hath to us, and that Spirit which worketh all things that are wrought according to the will of God, and that love wherewith we love God, and that love which we have to our neighbour, and that mercy and compassion which we shew on him, and also that eternal life which is laid up in store for us in Christ, are altogether the gift of God, through Christ's purchasing.

If the Scripture said always, Christ shall reward thee according to thy faith, or according to thy hope and trust thou hast in God, or according to the love thou hast to God and thy neighbour, so were it true also as thou seest, 1 Pet. i. Receiving the end or reward of our faith, the health or salvation of your souls. But the spiritual things could not be known save by their works, as a tree cannot be known but by her fruit.   How could I know that I loved my neighbour, if never occasion were given me to shew mercy unto him?

How we understand the love of God to be in us.

how should I know that I loved God, if I never suffered for his sake? how should I know that God loved me, if there were no infirmity, temptation, peril and jeopardy whence God should deliver me?

THERE is no man that forsaketh house, either father, or mother, either brethren or sisters, wife or children for the kingdom of heavens' sake, which shall not receive much more in this world, and in the world to come everlasting

Luke xviii.

life. (Luke xviii.)

Here seest thou that a Christian man in all his works hath respect to nothing, but unto the glory of God only, and to the maintaining of the truth of God, and doth, and leaveth undone all things of love, to the glory and

honour of God only, as Christ teacheth in the *Paternoster*.

Moreover when he saith, He shall receive much more
in this world, of a truth, yea he hath received much more
already.   For except he had felt the infinite mercy,
goodness, love, and kindness of God, and the fellowship
of the blood of Christ, and the comfort of the Spirit of
Christ in his heart, he could never have forsaken any thing
for God's sake.   Notwithstanding (as saith Mark x.)
Whosoever for Christ's sake and the gospel's, forsaketh
house, brethren or sisters &c. he shall receive an hundred fold houses, brethren &c. that is spiritually.   For
Christ shall be all things unto thee.   The angels, all
Christians, and whosoever doth the will of the father,
shall be father, mother, sister and brother unto thee, and
all theirs shall be thine.   And God shall take the care of
thee, and minister all things unto thee, as long as thou
seekest but his honour only.   Moreover if thou wert
Lord over all the world, yea, of ten worlds, before thou
knewest God; yet was not thine appetite quenched, thou
thirstedst for more.   But if thou seek his honour only,
then shall he slake thy thirst, and thou shalt have all that
thou desirest, and shall be content, yea if thou dwell
among infidels, and among the most cruel nations of
the world; yet shall he be a father unto thee, and shall
defend thee as he did Abraham, Isaac and Jacob, and all
saints whose lives thou readest in the Scripture.   For all
that are past and gone before are but ensamples to strengthen
our faith and trust in the word of God.   It is the same
God, and hath sworn to us all that he sware unto them,
and is as true as ever he was, and therefore cannot but fulfil his promises to us, as well as he did to them, if we
believe as they did.

The hour shall come when all they that are in the graves
shall hear his voice, that is to say, Christ's voice, and shall
come forth; they that have done good into the resurrection
of life, and they that have done evil into the resurrection of

Whosever for Christ's sake loseth any thing, shall receive an hundred fold.

If we once possess Christ by faith, then have we all in all, and are content with that we have.

69

damnation. (John v.) This, and all like texts, declare what followeth good works, and that our deeds shall testify with us, or against us at that day; and putteth us in remembrance to be diligent, and fervent in doing good. Hereby mayest thou not understand that we obtain the favour of God, and the inheritance of life, through the merits of good works, as hirelings do their wages. For then shouldest thou rob Christ, of whose fulness we have received favour for favour; (John i.) that is, God's favour was so full in Christ, that for his sake he giveth us his favour, as affirmeth also Paul, (Eph. i.) He loved us in his beloved, by whom we have (saith Paul) redemption through his blood, and forgiveness of sins. The forgiveness of sins, then, is our redemption in Christ, and not the reward of works. In whom (saith he in the same place) he chose us before the making of the world, that is long before we did good works. Through faith in Christ are we also the sons of God, as thou readest (John i.) In that they believed on his name, he gave them power to be the sons of God. God, with all his fulness and riches, dwelleth in Christ, and out of Christ must we fetch all things. Thou readest also (John iii.) He that believeth on the Son hath eternal life: and he that believeth not shall see no life, but the wrath of God abideth upon him. Here seest thou that the wrath and vengeance of God possesseth every man till faith come. Faith and trust in Christ expelleth the wrath of God, and bringeth favour, the Spirit, power to do good, and everlasting life. Moreover, until Christ hath given thee light, thou knowest not wherein standeth the goodness of thy works; and until his Spirit hath loosed thine heart, thou canst not consent unto good works. All that is good in us, both will and works, cometh of the favour of God, through Christ, to whom be all the laud. Amen.

IF any man will do his will (he meaneth the will of the Father,) he shall know of the doctrine whether it be of

70

God, or whether I speak of myself. (John vii.)   This John vii.
text meaneth not that any man of his own strength, power,
and free will, (as they call it,) can do the will of God
before he hath received the Spirit and strength of
Christ, through faith.   But here is meant that which is
spoken in the iiird of John, when Nicodemus marvelled
how it were possible that a man should be born again:
Christ answered, That which is born of the flesh is flesh,
and that which is born of the Spirit is Spirit; as who
should say, He that hath the Spirit through faith, and is
born again, and made anew in Christ, understandeth the
things of the Spirit, and what he that is spiritual meaneth.
But he that is flesh, and as Paul saith, (1 Cor. ii.) a natu- 1 Cor. ii.
ral man, and led of his blind reason only, can never
ascend to the capacity of the Spirit.   And he giveth an
ensample, saying, The wind bloweth where it listeth, and
thou hearest his voice, and wottest not whence he cometh,
nor whither he will: so is every man that is born of the The natu-
Spirit: he that speaketh of the Spirit can never be un- ral man, which is
derstood of the natural man, which is but flesh, and but flesh,
savoureth no more than things of the flesh.   So here favoureth not those
meaneth Christ, If any man have the Spirit, and con- things that are of the
senteth unto the will of God, this same at once wotteth Spirit.
what I mean.

IF ye understand these things, happy are ye if ye do
them. (John xiii.)   A Christian man's heart is with the John xiii.
will of God, with the law and commandments of God,
and hungereth and thirsteth after strength to fulfil them,
and mourneth day and night, desiring God, according to
his promises, for to give him power to fulfil the will of
God with love and lust: then testifieth his deed that he is
blessed, and that the Spirit which blesseth us in Christ is
in him, and ministereth such strength.   The outward deed
testifieth what is within us, as thou readest, (John v.) ·The John v.
deeds which I do testify of me, saith Christ.   And
(John xiii.) Hereby shall all men know that ye are my

71

disciples, if ye love one another. And (John xiv.) He that hath my commandments, and keepeth them, the same it is that loveth me. And again: He that loveth me keepeth my commandments; and he that loveth me not keepeth not my commandments: the outward deed testifieth of the inward heart. And (John xv.) If ye shall keep my commandments ye shall continue in my love, as I keep my Father's commandment, and continue in his love. That is, As ye see the love that I have to my Father, in that I keep his commandments, so shall ye see the love that ye have to me, in that ye keep my commandments.

Thou mayest not think that our deeds bless us first, and that we prevent God and his grace in Christ, as though we, in our natural gifts, and being as we were born in Adam, looked on the law of God, and of our own strength fulfilled it, and so became righteous, and then, with that righteousness, obtained the favour of God. As philosophers write of righteousness, and as the righteousness of temporal law is, where the law is satisfied with the hypocrisy of the outward deed. For contrary to that readest thou

(John xv.) Ye have not chosen me (saith Christ,) but I have chosen you, that ye go and bring forth fruit, and that your fruit remain. And in the same chapter: I am a vine, and ye the branches; and without me can ye do nothing. With us, therefore, so goeth it. In Adam are we all, as it were, wild crab-trees, of which God chooseth whom he will, and plucketh them out of Adam, and planteth them in the garden of his mercy, and stocketh them, and grafteth the Spirit of Christ in them, which bringeth forth the fruit of the will of God; which fruit testifieth that God hath blessed us in Christ. Note this also; that as long as we live we are yet partly carnal and fleshly, (notwithstanding that we are in Christ, and though it be not imputed unto us for Christ's sake,) for there abideth and remaineth in us yet of the old Adam, as it were of the stock of the crab-tree; and ever among, when occasion is given him, shooteth forth his branches and leaves, bud, blossom, and fruit: against whom we must fight and subdue him, and change all his nature by a little and a little, with prayer, fasting, and watching; with virtuous meditation and holy works, until we be altogether spirit. The kingdom of heaven, saith Christ, (Matt. xiii.) is like leaven, which a woman taketh and hideth in three pecks of meal till all be leavened. The leaven is the Spirit, and we the meal, which must be seasoned with the Spirit a little and a little, till we be throughout spiritual.

Which shall reward every man according to his deed; (Rom. ii.) That is, according as the deeds are so shall every man's reward be: the deeds declare what we are, as the fruit the tree; according to the fruit shall the tree be praised. The reward is given of the mercy and truth of God, and by the deserving and merits of Christ. Whosoever repenteth, believeth the gospel, and putteth his trust in Christ's merits, the same is heir with Christ of eternal life; for assurance whereof, the Spirit of God is poured into his heart as an earnest, which looseth him from the bonds of Satan, and giveth him lust and strength every day more and more, according as he is diligent to ask of God for Christ's sake: and eternal life followeth good living. I suppose, (saith St. Paul in the same epistle, the viiith chapter,) that the afflictions of this world are not worthy of the glory which shall be shewed on us; that is to say, that which we here suffer can never deserve that reward which there shall be given us.

Moreover, if the reward should depend and hang of the works, no man should be saved: forasmuch as our best deeds, compared to the law, are damnable sin. By the deeds of the law is no flesh justified, as it is written in the third chapter to the Romans. The law justifieth not, but uttereth the sin only, and compelleth and driveth the penitent, or repenting sinner, to flee unto the sanctuary of mercy in the blood of Christ. Also repent we never so much, be we never so well willing unto the law of God, yet are we so weak, and the snares and occasions so innumerable, that we fall daily and hourly: so that we could not but despair if the reward hanged of the work. Whosoever ascribeth eternal life unto the deserving and merit of works, must fall in one of two inconveniences; either must he be a blind Pharisee, not seeing that the law is spiritual and he carnal, and look and rejoice in the outward shining of his deeds, despising the weak, and, in respect of them, justify himself; or else (if he see how that the law is spiritual, and he never able to ascend unto that which the law requireth,) he must needs despair.

Christ is our hope and righteousness. Let every Christian man, therefore, rejoice in Christ our hope, trust, and righteousness, in whom we are loved, chosen, and accepted unto the inheritance of eternal life; neither presuming in our perfectness, neither despairing in our weakness. The perfecter a man is the clearer is his sight, and seeth a thousand things which displease him, and also perfectness that cannot be obtained in this life; and therefore desireth to be with Christ, where **Let no man despair, but put his hope in Christ and he shall be safe.** is no more sin. Let him that is weak and cannot do that he would fain do, not despair, but turn to Him that is strong, and hath promised to give strength to all that ask of him in Christ's name; and complain to God, and desire him to fulfil his promises, and to God commit himself; and he shall of his mercy and truth strengthen him, and make him feel with what love he is beloved for Christ's sake, though he be never so weak.

Rom. ii. THEY are not righteous before God which hear the law; but they which do the law shall be justified. (Rom. ii.) This text is plainer than that it needeth to be expounded. In the chapter before, Paul proveth that the law natural holp not the Gentiles, (as appeareth by the law, statutes, and ordinances which they made in their cities,) yet kept they them not. The great keep the small under, for their own profit, with the violence of the law. Every man praiseth the law as far forth as it is profitable and pleasant unto himself. But when his own appetites should be refrained, then grudgeth he against the law. Moreover, he proveth that no knowledge holp the Gentiles. For though the learned men (as the philosophers,) came to the knowledge of God by the creatures of the world, yet had they no power to worship God. In this second chapter proveth he that the Jews, (though they had the law written,) yet it holp them not: they could not keep it, but were idolaters, and were also murderers, adulterers, and whatsoever the law forbad. He concludeth, therefore, that the Jew is as well damned as the Gentile. If hearing of the law only might have justified, then had the Jews been righteous. But it requireth that a man do the law if he will be righteous; which, because the Jew did not, he is no less damned than the Gentile. The publishing and declaring of the law doth but utter a man's sin, and giveth neither strength nor help to fulfil the law. The law killeth thy conscience, and giveth thee no lust to fulfil the law. Faith in Christ giveth lust and power to do the law. Now, is it true, that he which doth the law is righteous, but that doth no man save he that believeth and putteth his trust in Christ.

No man can fulfil the law but he that believeth in Christ.

If any man's work that he hath built upon abide, he shall receive a reward. (1 Cor. ii.) The circumstance of the same chapter, that is to wit, that which goeth before and that which followeth, declareth plainly what is meant. Paul talketh of learning, doctrine, or preaching: he saith that he himself hath laid the foundation, which is Jesus Christ, and that no man can lay any other. He exhorteth, therefore, every man to take heed what he buildeth upon; and borroweth a similitude of the goldsmith which trieth his metals with fire, saying that the fire, that is, the judgment of the Scripture, shall try every man's work, that is, every man's preaching and doctrine. If any build upon the foundation laid of Paul, I mean Jesus Christ, gold, silver, or precious stone, which are all one thing, and signify true doctrine, which, when it is exa-

1 Cor. ii.

Christ is the sure foundation.

75

mined, the Scripture alloweth ; then shall he have his reward, that is, he shall be sure that his learning is of God,
and that God's Spirit is in him, and that he shall have the
reward that Christ hath purchased for him.　On the other
side, if any man build thereon timber, hay, or stubble,
which are all one, and signify doctrine of man's imagination, traditions, and fantasies, which stand not with Christ
when they are judged and examined by the Scripture, he
shall suffer damage, but shall be saved himself, yet as it
were through fire ; that is, it shall be painful unto him
that he hath lost his labour, and to see his building perish ;
notwithstanding, if he repent, and embrace the truth in
Christ, he shall obtain mercy and be saved.　But if Paul
were now alive, and would defend his own learning, he
should be tried through fire ; not through fire of the
judgment of Scripture, (for that light men now utterly
refuse,) but by the Pope's law, and with fire of fagots.

Man's foundation is feeble.

WE must all appear before the judgment-seat of Christ,
for to receive every man according to the deeds of his
body : (2 Cor. v.)　As thy deeds testify of thee so shall thy
reward be.　Thy deeds be evil, then is the wrath of God
upon thee, and thine heart is evil ; and so shall thy reward
be, if thou repent not.　Fear, therefore, and cry to God
for grace, that thou mayest love his laws.　And when
thou lovest them, cease not till thou have obtained power
of God to fulfil them ; so shalt thou be sure that a good
reward shall follow.　Which reward, not thy deeds, but
Christ's have purchased for thee ; whose purchasing also
is that lust which thou hast to God's law, and that might
wherewith thou fulfillest them.　Remember also, that a
reward is rather called that which is given freely, than that
which is deserved.　That which is deserved is called (if
thou wilt give him his right name,) hire or wages.　A
reward is given freely, to provoke unto love and to make
friends.

2 Cor. v.

Christ re-wardeth his own works in us.

Remember, that whatsoever good thing any man doth,

that shall he receive of the Lord : (Eph. vi.) remembering that ye shall receive of the Lord the reward of inheritance. (Col. iii.) These two texts are exceeding plain. Paul meaneth, as Peter doth, (1 Pet. ii.) that servants should obey their masters with all their hearts, and with good will, though they were never so evil. Yea, he will that all who are under power obey, even of heart, and of conscience to God, because God will have it so, be the rulers never so wicked. The children must obey father and mother, be they never so cruel or unkind ; likewise the wife her husband, the servant his master, the subjects and commons their lord or king. Why ? For ye serve the Lord, saith he in Coloss. iii. We are Christ's, and Christ has bought us, as thou readest Rom. xiv. 1 Cor. vi. 1 Pet. i. Christ is our Lord, and we his possession, and his also is the commandment. Now, ought not the cruelness and churlishness of father and mother, of husband, master, lord, or king, cause us to hate the commandment of our so kind a Lord Christ ; which spared not his blood for our sakes ; which also hath purchased for us with his blood that reward of eternal life, which life shall follow the patience of good living, and whereunto our good deeds testify that we are chosen. Furthermore, we are so carnal, that if the rulers be good, we cannot know whether we keep the commandment for the love that we have to Christ, and to God through him, or no. But and if thou canst find in thine heart, to do good unto him that rewardeth thee evil again, then art thou sure that the same Spirit is in thee that is in Christ. And it followeth in the same chapter to the Colossians, He that doth wrong shall receive for the wrong that he hath done. That is, God shall avenge thee abundantly, which seeth what wrong is done unto thee, and yet suffereth it for a time, that thou mightest feel thy patience and the working of his Spirit in thee, and be made perfect. Therefore, see that thou not once desire vengeance, but remit all vengeance unto God, as Christ did, which saith Peter, (1 Pet. ii.) when

Eph. vi.

Coloss. iii.

We must obey the magistrates, because God will have it so.

Rom. xiv.
1 Cor. vi.
1 Pet. i.

A good lesson to teach us to know when we have the Spirit of God.

Remit all vengeance to God.

he was reviled, reviled not again, neither threatened when he suffered. Unto such obedience, unto such patience, unto such a poor heart, and unto such feeling, is Paul's meaning to bring all men, and not unto the vain disputing of them that ascribe so high a place in heaven unto their pilled merits; which, as they feel not the working of God's Spirit, so obey they no man. If the king do unto *The fury of the Popish clergy.* them but right, they will interdict the whole realm, curse, excommunicate, and send them down far beneath the bottom of hell, as they have brought the people out of their wits, and made them mad to believe.

Acts x.   THY prayers and alms are come up into remembrance in the presence of God; (in the Acts x.) that is, God forgetteth thee not, though he cometh not at the first calling, he looketh on and beholdeth thy prayers and alms. Prayer cometh from the heart. God looketh first on the heart and then on the deed, as thou readest (Gen. iv.) God beheld or looked first on Abel, and then on his offering. If the heart be unpure the deed verily pleaseth not, as thou seest in Cain. Mark the order, in the beginning of the chapter thou readest; There was a certain man named *Cornelius* which feared God, gave much alms, and prayed God alway. He feared God, that is, he trembled and quaked to break the commandments of God. Then prayed *Prayer is the fruit of faith.* he alway. Prayer is the fruit, effect, deed or act of faith, and is nothing but the longing of the heart for those things which a man lacketh, and which God hath promised to give him. He doth also alms, alms is the fruit, effect, or deed of compassion and pity which we have to our neighbour. O a glorious faith and a right which so trusteth God, and believeth *Lively faith is not without works.* his promises, that she feareth to break his commandments, and is also merciful unto her neighbour! This is that faith whereof thou readest, namely in Peter, Paul, and John, that we are thereby both justified and saved, and whosoever imagineth any other faith deceiveth himself and is a vain disputer, and a brawler about words, and hath no feeling in his heart.

78

Though thou consent to the law, that it is good, righteous, and holy, sorrowest and repentest, because thou hast broken it, mournest because thou hast no strength to fulfil it, yet art not thou thereby at one with God: yea, thou shouldest shortly despair and blaspheme God, if the promises of forgiveness and of help were not thereby, and faith in thine heart to believe them; faith therefore setteth thee at one with God.

Faith prayeth always. For she hath always her infirmities and weaknesses before her eyes, and also God's promises, for which she always longeth, and in all places. But blind unbelief prayeth not alway, nor in all places, but in the church only, and that in such a church where it is not lawful to preach God's promises, neither to teach men to trust therein. Faith, when she prayeth, setteth not her good deeds before her, saying, Lord, for my good deeds do this or that; nor bargaineth with God, saying, Lord, grant me this, or do this or that, and I will do this or that for thee; as mumble so much daily, go so far, or fast this or that fast, enter this religion or that, with such other points of infidelity, yea, rather idolatry; but she setteth her infirmities and her lack before her face, and God's promises, saying, Lord, for thy mercy and truth which thou hast sworn, be merciful unto me, and pluck me out of this prison and out of this hell, and loose the bonds of Satan, and give me power to glorify thy name: faith therefore justifieth in the heart and before God, and the deeds justify outwardly before the world, that is, testify only before men, what we are inwardly before God.

Whosoever looketh in the perfect law of liberty and continueth therein, (if he be not a forgetful hearer, but a doer of the work) he shall be happy in his deed: (James i.) The law of liberty, that is, which requireth a free heart, or if thou fulfil it, declareth a free heart, loosed from the bonds of Satan. The preaching of the law maketh no man free, but bindeth, for it is the key that bindeth all conciences unto eternal damnation, when it is preached; as the pro-

Faith maketh us at one with God.

Faith prayeth always and in all places.

The prayer of a faithful man.

James i.

79

mises or gospel is the key that looseth all consiences that repent, when they are bound through preaching of the law. He shall be happy in his deed, that is, by his deed shall he know that he is happy and blessed of God, which hath given him a good heart, and power to fulfil the law; by hearing the law thou shalt not know that thou art blessed, but if thou do it, it declareth that thou art happy and blessed.

WAS not Abraham justified of his deeds when he offered James iii. his son Isaac upon the altar? (James iii.) His deed justified him before the world, that is, it declared and uttered the faith which both justified him before God, and wrought that wonderful work, as James also affirmeth.

Was not Rahab the harlot justified when she received the messengers, and sent them out another way? (James iii.) That is likewise outwardly, but before God she was justified by faith which wrought that outward deed, as thou mayest see, Josh. ii. She had heard what God had done in Egypt, in the red sea, in the desert, and unto the two kings of the Amoreans, Sihon and Og. And she confessed saying, Your Lord God, he is God in heaven above and in earth beneath. She also believed that God, as he had promised the children of Israel, would give them the land wherein she dwelt; and consented thereunto, submitted herself unto the will of God, and holp God, (as much as in her was) and saved his spies and messengers. The other feared that which she believed, but resisted God with all their might, and had no power to submit themselves unto the will of God. And therefore perished they, and she was saved and that through faith : as we read Heb. xi. where thou mayest see how the holy fathers were saved through faith, and

Faith is the goodness of all the deeds that are done within the law of God. how faith wrought in them. Faith is the goodness of all the deeds that are done within the law of God, and maketh them good and glorious, seem they never so vile; and unbelief maketh them damnable, seem they never so glorious.

James iii. As pertaining to that which James in this iiird chapter

saith, What availeth though a man say that he hath faith
if he have no deeds? can faith save him? and again, faith
without deeds is dead in itself; and the devils believe and
tremble: and as the body without the spirit is dead, even
so faith without deeds is dead; it is manifest and clear,
that he meaneth not of the faith whereof Peter and Paul
speak in their epistles. John in his gospel and first epistle,
and Christ in the gospel, when he saith, Thy faith hath
made thee safe, be it to thee according to thy faith, or
great is thy faith, and so forth; and of which James himself speaketh in the first chapter, saying, Of his own will
begat he us with the word of life, that is, in believing the
the promises wherein is life, are we made the sons of
God.

Which thing I also thiswise prove: Paul saith how
shall or can they believe without a preacher? how should
they preach except they were sent? Now I pray you when
was it heard that God sent any man to preach unto the
devils, or that he made them any good promise? He threat-
eneth them oft, but never sent any ambassadors to preach
any atonement between him and them. Take an ensample
that thou mayest understand: let there be two poor men
both destitute of rayment in a cold winter, the one strong
that he feeleth no grief, the other grievously mourning for
pain of the cold. I then come by, and, moved with pity and
compassion, say unto him that feeleth his disease, Come to
such a plac eand I will give thee raiment sufficient. He
believeth, cometh and obtaineth that which I have promised.
That other seeth all this and knoweth it, but is partaker of
nought, for he hath no faith, and that is because there is
no promise made him. So is it of the devils, the devils have
no faith, for faith is but earnest believing of God's
promises. Now are there no promises made unto the devils, but sore threatenings. The old philosophers knew that
there was one God, but yet had no faith, for they had
no power to seek his will, neither to worship him. The
Turks and the Saracens know that there is one God, but

An exam-
ple.

Turks have
no faith
and yet
know there
is a God.

81

yet have no faith, for they have no power to worship God
in spirit, to seek his pleasure, and to submit them unto his
will. They made an idol of God, (as we do for the most
part) and worshipped him every man after his own imagination, and for a sundry purpose. What we will have
done, that must God do, and to do our will worship we
hymn and pray unto him; but what God will have done,
that will neither Turk nor Saracen, nor the most part of us
do. Whatsoever we imagine righteous, that must God admit; but God's righteousness will not our hearts admit.

An example. Take another ensample: let there be two such as I spake
of before, and I promise both, and the one because he
feeleth not his disease cometh not: so is it of God's
promises: no man is holpen by them but sinners that feel
their sins, mourn and sorrow for them, and repent with
all their hearts. For John Baptist went before Christ and
preached repentance, that is, he preached the law of God
right, and brought the people into knowledge of themselves, and unto the fear of God, and then sent them unto
Christ to be healed. For in Christ and for his sake only,
hath God promised to receive us unto mercy, to forgive us,
and to give us power to resist sin. How shall God save
thee, when thou knowest not thy damnation? how shall
Christ deliver thee from sin, when thou wilt not knowledge thy sin? Now I pray thee how many thousands are
there of them that say, I believe that Christ was born of
a virgin, that he died, that he rose again, and so forth, and
thou canst not bring them in belief that they have any sin
at all! How many are there of the same sort, which thou
canst not make believe that a thousand things are sin which
God damneth for sin all the Scripture throughout! as to
Sins that are exemped no sins. buy as good cheap as he can, and to sell as dear as he can,
to raise the market of corn and victuals for his own vantage,
without respect of his neighbour, or of the poor of the common wealth, and such like. Moreover how many hundred
thousand are there, which when they have sinned, and
knowledge their sins; yet trust in a bald ceremony, or in

82

a lousy friar's coat and merits, or in the prayers of them
that devour widows' houses, and eateth the poor out of
house and harbour, in a thing of his own imagination, in
a foolish dream, and a false vision; and not in Christ's
blood, and in the truth that God hath sworn! All these
are faithless, for they follow their own righteousness, and
are disobedient unto all manner [of] righteousness of
God: both unto the righteousness of God's law, wherewith he damneth all our deeds, (for though some of them
see their sins for fear of pain, yet had they rather that
such deeds were no sin,) and also unto the righteousness
of the truth of God in his promises, whereby he saveth
all that repent and believe them. For though they believe
that Christ died, yet believe they not that he died for their
sins, and that his death is a sufficient satisfaction for
their sins, and that God for his sake will be a father unto
them, and give them power to resist sin.

Paul saith to the Romans in the xth chapter, If thou
confess with thy mouth that Jesus is the Lord, and
believe with thine heart that God raised him up from
death, thou shalt be safe. That is, if thou believe he
raised him up again for thy salvation. Many believe
that God is rich and almighty, but not unto themselves,
and that he will be good unto them, and defend them,
and be their God.

Pharaoh for pain of the plague, was compelled to
confess his sins, but had yet no power to submit himself
unto the will of God, and to let the children of Israel
go, and to lose so great profit for God's pleasure, As
our prelates confess their sins, saying, Though we be never
so evil, yet have we the power. And again, the scribes
and pharisees (say they) sat in Moses's seat, do as they
teach, but not as they do; thus confess they that they are
abominable. But to the second I answer, if they sat on
Christ's seat they would preach Christ's doctrine, now
preach they their own traditions, and therefore not to be
heard. If they preached Christ, we ought to hear them

Faithless fruits.

Rom. x.

Pharaoh confessed his sins.

83

though they were never so abominable, as they of themselves confess, and have yet no power to amend, neither to let loose Christ's flock to serve God in the Spirit, which they hold captive, compelling them to serve their

The devils confessed Christ to be the Son of God.

false lies. The devils felt the power of Christ, and were compelled against their wills to confess that he was the Son of God, but had no power to be content therewith, neither to consent unto the ordinance and eternal counsel of the everlasting God; as our prelates feel the power of God against them, but yet have no grace to give room unto Christ, because that they (as the devil's nature is) will themselves sit in his holy temple, that is to wit, the consciences of men.

Simon Magus's faith.

Simon Magus believed, (Acts. iii.) with such a faith as the devils confessed Christ, but had no right faith, as thou seest in the said chapter. For he repented not, consenting unto the law of God. Neither believed the promises or longed for them, but wondered only at the miracles which Philip wrought, and because that he himself in Philip's presence had no power to use his witchcraft, sorcery and art magic, wherewith he mocked and deluded the wits of the people. He would have bought the gift of God, to have sold it much dearer, as his successors now do, and not the successors of Simon Peter. For were they Simon Peter's successors, they would preach Christ as he did ; but they are Simon Magus's successors,

2 Pet ii.

of which Simon Peter well prophesied in the second chapter of his second Epistle, saying, There were false prophets among the people (meaning of the Jews) even as there shall be false teachers or doctors among you, which privily shall bring in sects damnable, (sects is part-taking, as one holdeth of Francis, another of Dominic, which thing also

1 Cor. i. 3.

Paul rebuketh, 1 Cor. i. and iii.) even denying the Lord that bought them (for they will not be saved by Christ, neither suffer any man to preach him to other.) And many shall follow their damnable ways, (thou wilt say, Shall God suffer so many to go out of the right way so long? I answer, many must follow their damnable ways, or else must Peter be a false prophet) by which the way of truth shall be evil spoken of, (as it is now at this present time, for it is heresy to preach the truth) and through covetousness shall they with feigned words make merchandise of you. Of their merchandise and covetousness it needeth not to make rehearsal, for they that be blind see it evidently.

Thus seest thou that James, when he saith, Faith without deeds is dead, and as the body without the spirit is dead, so is faith without deeds, and the devils believe; that he meaneth not of the faith and trust that we have in the truth of God's promises, and his holy Testament, made unto us in Christ's blood; which faith followeth repentance, and the consent of the heart unto the law of God, and maketh a man safe, and setteth him at peace with God. But speaketh of that false opinion and imagination wherewith some say, I believe that Christ was born of a virgin, and that he died, and so forth. That believe they verily, and so strongly, that they are ready to slay whosoever would say the contrary. But they believe not that Christ died for their sins, and that his death hath appeased the wrath of God, and hath obtained for them all that God hath promised in the Scripture. For how can they believe that Christ died for their sins, and that he is their only and sufficient Saviour, seeing that they seek other Saviours of their own imagination, and seeing that they feel not their sins, neither repent, except that some repent (as I above said) for fear of pain, but for no love, nor consent unto the law of God, nor longing that they have for those good promises which he hath made them in Christ's blood. If they repented and loved the law of God, and longed for that help which God hath promised to give to all that call on him for Christ's sake, then verily must God's truth give them power and strength to do good works, whensoever occasion were given, either must God be a false God. But let God be true, and every man a liar as Scripture saith. For the truth of God lasteth ever, to whom only be all honour and glory for ever. Amen.

An epitome or brief recital of that which is entreated of before.

Be not offended, most dear reader, that divers things are overseen, through negligence in this little treatise. For verily the chance was such, that I marvel that it is so well as it is. Moreover it becometh the book even so to come as a mourner, and in vile apparel to wait on his master, which sheweth himself now again, not in honour and glory, as between Moses and Elias; but in rebuke and shame, as between two murderers, to try his true friends, and to prove whether there be any faith on the earth.

Also from Benediction Books ...

Wandering Between Two Worlds: Essays on Faith and Art
Anita Mathias
Benediction Books, 2007
152 pages
ISBN: 0955373700

Available from www.amazon.com, www.amazon.co.uk
www.wanderingbetweentwoworlds.com

In these wide-ranging lyrical essays, Anita Mathias writes, in lush, lovely prose, of her naughty Catholic childhood in Jamshedpur, India; her large, eccentric family in Mangalore, a sea-coast town converted by the Portuguese in the sixteenth century; her rebellion and atheism as a teenager in her Himalayan boarding school, run by German missionary nuns, St. Mary's Convent, Nainital; and her abrupt religious conversion after which she entered Mother Teresa's convent in Calcutta as a novice. Later rich, elegant essays explore the dualities of her life as a writer, mother, and Christian in the United States-- Domesticity and Art, Writing and Prayer, and the experience of being "an alien and stranger" as an immigrant in America, sensing the need for roots.

About the Author

Anita Mathias was born in India, has a B.A. and M.A. in English from Somerville College, Oxford University and an M.A. in Creative Writing from the Ohio State University. Her essays have been published in The Washington Post, The London Magazine, The Virginia Quarterly Review, Commonweal, Notre Dame Magazine, America, The Christian Century, Religion Online, The Southwest Review, Contemporary Literary Criticism, New Letters, The Journal, and two of HarperSanFrancisco's The Best Spiritual Writing anthologies. Her non-fiction has won fellowships from The National Endowment for the Arts; The Minnesota State Arts Board; The Jerome Foundation, The Vermont Studio Center; The Virginia Centre for the Creative Arts, and the First Prize for the Best General Interest Article from the Catholic Press Association of the United States and Canada. Anita has taught Creative Writing at the College of William and Mary, and now lives and writes in Oxford, England.

Religio Medici, Hydriotaphia, Letter to a Friend, Thomas Browne

Pseudodoxia Epidemica: Or, Enquiries into Commonly Presumed Truths, Thomas Browne

Urne Buriall and The Garden of Cyrus, Thomas Browne

The Maid's Tragedy, Beaumont and Fletcher

The Custom of the Country, Beaumont and Fletcher

Philaster Or Love Lies a Bleeding, Beaumont and Fletcher

A Treatise of Fishing with an Angle, Dame Juliana Berners.

Pamphilia to Amphilanthus, Lady Mary Wroth

The Compleat Angler, Izaak Walton

The Magnetic Lady, Ben Jonson

Every Man Out of His Humour, Ben Jonson

The Masque of Blacknesse. The Masque of Beauty,. Ben Jonson

The Life of St. Thomas More, William Roper

Pendennis, William Makepeace Thackeray

Salmacis and Hermaphroditus attributed to Francis Beaumont

Friar Bacon and Friar Bungay Robert Greene

Holy Wisdom, Augustine Baker

The Jew of Malta and the Massacre at Paris, Christopher Marlowe

Tamburlaine the Great, Parts 1 & 2 AND Massacre at Paris, Christopher Marlowe

All Ovids Elegies, Lucans First Booke, Dido Queene of Carthage, Hero and Leander, Christopher Marlowe

The Titan, Theodore Dreiser

Scapegoats of the Empire: The true story of the Bushveldt Carbineers, George Witton

All Hallows' Eve, Charles Williams

The Place of The Lion, Charles Williams

The Greater Trumps, Charles Williams

My Apprenticeship: Volumes I and II, Beatrice Webb

Last and First Men / Star Maker, Olaf Stapledon

Last and First Men, Olaf Stapledon

Darkness and the Light, Olaf Stapledon

The Worst Journey in the World, Apsley Cherry-Garrard

The Schoole of Abuse, Containing a Pleasaunt Invective Against Poets, Pipers, Plaiers, Iesters and Such Like Catepillers of the Commonwelth, Stephen Gosson

Russia in the Shadows, H. G. Wells

Wild Swans at Coole, W. B. Yeats

A hundreth good pointes of husbandrie, Thomas Tusser

The Collected Works of Nathanael West: "The Day of the Locust", "The Dream Life of Balso Snell", "Miss Lonelyhearts", "A Cool Million", Nathanael West

Miss Lonelyhearts & The Day of the Locust, Nathaniel West

The Worst Journey in the World, Apsley Cherry-Garrard

Scott's Last Expedition, V1, R. F. Scott

The Dream of Gerontius, John Henry Newman

The Brother of Daphne, Dornford Yates

The Downfall of Robert Earl of Huntington, Anthony Munday

Clayhanger, Arnold Bennett

The Regent, A Five Towns Story Of Adventure In London, Arnold Bennett

The Card, A Story Of Adventure In The Five Towns, Arnold Bennett

South: The Story of Shackleton's Last Expedition 1914-1917, Sir Ernest Shackketon

Greene's Groatsworth of Wit: Bought With a Million of Repentance, Robert Greene

Beau Sabreur, Percival Christopher Wren

The Hekatompathia, or Passionate Centurie of Love, Thomas Watson

The Art of Rhetoric, Thomas Wilson

Stepping Heavenward, Elizabeth Prentiss

Barker's Delight, or The Art of Angling, Thomas Barker

The Napoleon of Notting Hill, G.K. Chesterton

The Douay-Rheims Bible (The Challoner Revision)

Endimion - The Man in the Moone, John Lyly

Gallathea and Midas, John Lyly,

Mother Bombie, John Lyly

Manners, Custom and Dress During the Middle Ages and During the Renaissance Period, Paul Lacroix

Obedience of a Christian Man, William Tyndale

St. Patrick for Ireland, James Shirley

The Wrongs of Woman; Or Maria/Memoirs of the Author of a Vindication of the Rights of Woman, Mary Wollstonecraft and William Godwin

De Adhaerendo Deo. Of Cleaving to God, Albertus Magnus

Obedience of a Christian Man, William Tyndale

A Trick to Catch the Old One, Thomas Middleton

The Phoenix, Thomas Middleton

A Yorkshire Tragedy, Thomas Middleton (attrib.)

The Princely Pleasures at Kenelworth Castle, George Gascoigne

The Fair Maid of the West. Part I and Part II. Thomas Heywood

Proserpina, Volume I and Volume II. Studies of Wayside Flowers, John Ruskin

Our Fathers Have Told Us. Part I. The Bible of Amiens. John Ruskin

The Poetry of Architecture: Or the Architecture of the Nations of Europe Considered in Its Association with Natural Scenery and National Character, John Ruskin

The Endeavour Journal of Sir Joseph Banks. Sir Joseph Banks

Christ Legends: And Other Stories, Selma Lagerlof; (trans. Velma Swanston Howard)

Chamber Music, James Joyce

Blurt, Master Constable, Thomas Middleton, Thomas Dekker

Since Yesterday, Frederick Lewis Allen

The Scholemaster: Or, Plaine and Perfite Way of Teachyng Children the Latin Tong , Roger Ascham

The Wonderful Year, 1603, Thomas Dekker

Waverley, Sir Walter Scott

Guy Mannering, Sir Walter Scott

Old Mortality, Sir Walter Scott

The Knight of Malta, John Fletcher

The Double Marriage, John Fletcher and Philip Massinger

Space Prison, Tom Godwin

The Home of the Blizzard Being the Story of the Australasian Antarctic Expedition, 1911-1914, Douglas Mawson

Wild-goose Chase , John Fletcher

If You Know Not Me, You Know Nobody. Part I and Part II, Thomas Heywood

The Ragged Trousered Philanthropists, Robert Tressell

The Island of Sheep, John Buchan

Eyes of the Woods, Joseph Altsheler

The Club of Queer Trades, G. K. Chesterton

The Financier, Theodore Dreiser

Something of Myself, Rudyard Kipling

Law of Freedom in a Platform, or True Magistracy Restored, Gerrard Winstanley

Damon and Pithias, Richard Edwards

Dido Queen of Carthage: And, The Massacre at Paris, Christopher Marlowe

Cocoa and Chocolate: Their History from Plantation to Consumer, Arthur Knapp

Lady of Pleasure, James Shirley

The South Pole: An account of the Norwegian Antarctic expedition in the "Fram," 1910-12. Volume 1 and Volume 2, Roald Amundsen

A Yorkshire Tragedy, Thomas Middleton (attrib.)

The Tragedy of Soliman and Perseda, Thomas Kyd

The Rape of Lucrece. Thomas Heywood

Myths and Legends of Ancient Greece and Rome, E. M. Berens

In the Forbidden Land, Henry Savage Arnold Landor

Across Unknown South America, by Arnold Henry Savage Landor

Illustrated History of Furniture: From the Earliest to the Present Time, Frederick Litchfield

A Narrative of Some of the Lord's Dealings with George Müller Written by Himself (Parts I-IV, 1805-1856), George Müller

The Towneley Cycle Of The Mystery Plays (Or The Wakefield Cycle): Thirty-Two Pageants, Anonymous

The Insatiate Countesse, John Marston.

Spontaneous Activity in Education, Maria Montessori.

On the Art of Writing, Sir Arthur Quiller-Couch

The Well of the Saints, J. M. Synge

Bacon's Advancement Of Learning And The New Atlantis, Francis Bacon.

Catholic Tales And Christian Songs, Dorothy Sayers.

Two Little Savages: Being the Adventures of Two Boys who Lived as Indians and What they Learned, Ernest Thompson Seton

The Sadness of Christ, Thomas More

The Family of Love, Thomas Middleton

The Passing of the Aborigines: A Lifetime Spent Among the Natives of Australia, Daisy Bates

The Children, Edith Wharton

A Record of European Armour and Arms through Seven Centuries., Francis Laking

The Book of the Farm: - Detailing The Labours Of The Farmer, Steward, Plowman, Hedger, Cattle-Man, Shepherd, Field-Worker, and Dairymaid. (Volume I). by Henry Stephens

The Book of the Farm: - Detailing The Labours Of The Farmer, Steward, Plowman, Hedger, Cattle-Man, Shepherd, Field-Worker, and Dairymaid. (Volume II). by Henry Stephens

The Book of the Farm: - Detailing The Labours Of The Farmer, Steward, Plowman, Hedger, Cattle-Man, Shepherd, Field-Worker, and Dairymaid. (Volume III). by Henry Stephens

The Naturalist On The River Amazons, by Henry Walter Bates

and many others…

Tell us what you would love to see in print again, at affordable prices! Email: **benedictionbooks@btinternet.com**

CPSIA information can be obtained at www.ICGtesting.com
Printed in the USA
LVOW07*0033040414

380186LV00005B/303/P

9 781849 029995